Mushroon
Other Fⁱ
of Britaın
& Northern Europe

A NATURALIST'S GUIDE TO THE

Mushrooms and Other Fungi of Britain
& Northern Europe

Josephine Bacon, Paul Sterry & Andrew Merrick

BEAUFOY BOOKS

First published in the United Kingdom in 2010 by Beaufoy Books
11 Blenheim Court, 316 Woodstock Road, Oxford OX2 7NS, England
www.johnbeaufoy.com

10 9 8 7 6 5 4 3 2

ISBN 978-1-906780-16-6

COVER PICTURES
Front cover: *top left* Shaggy Inkcap; *top right* Glistening Inkcap;
bottom left Common Puffball; *bottom middle* Blackening Waxcap;
bottom right Yellow Staghorn.
Back cover: Orange Peel Fungus.

DISCLAIMER
**Great care has been taken to maintain the accuracy of
the information contained in this work. However, neither
the publisher nor the author can be held responsible for
any consequences arising from use of the information
contained herein.**

Edited, designed and typeset by
D & N Publishing, Baydon, Wiltshire, UK

Printed and bound in Malaysia by Times Offset (M) Sdn. Bhd.

·CONTENTS·

An Introduction to the Larger Fungi

Fungi were once classified as flowerless plants (cryptogams) along with ferns, mosses and algae because, like them, they produce spores as opposed to seeds. They are now placed in their own separate kingdom – larger than those of plants or animals – containing an estimated 1.5 million species. In fact, fungi are believed to be more closely related to animals than plants, since they inhale oxygen, exhale carbon dioxide and cannot photosynthesise; in fact, they are not generally sensitive to light, which is why they are able to grow in the dark. Their food is derived from breaking down nutrients that may be in the soil or in other plants, even in other fungi and animals (including humans). Their similarity to the animal kingdom is such that there is a group of moulds, once considered fungi, known as the slime moulds (myxomycetes), that actually move, albeit very slowly (one example, Wolf's Milk, is included in this book on p. 155).

Fungi that live off dead matter are called saprophytes, while those that feed on living plants and animals are called parasites. Fungi are able to digest all types of living and dead matter and can extract minerals from the soil, even from rocks. Some of the fungi that live on wood can be both saprophytic and parasitic. There are also symbiotic fungi, which live in conjunction with certain plants, feeding from them and in turn supplying them with nutrients. The fungi are extremely valuable in forestry, as they help trees to grow by enabling them to absorb nutrients that they could not obtain in any other way.

Fungi can also be serious and deadly plant pests – the Potato Blight *Phytophthora infestans* and the Coffee Leaf Rust *Hemileia vastatrix* are just two examples. Dry rot *Serpula lacrymans* destroys the timber of houses, while aflatoxins (the poisons produced by certain moulds) can kill humans and animals. On the other hand, fungi are great producers of antibiotics and killers of bacteria, and they are used in the creation of statins, medicines now widely prescribed to reduce cholesterol. Fungi also have potential uses in the control of major pollutants, such as oil spills and contaminated agricultural waste. The yeasts are fungi and have been used for thousands of years to leaven bread and make beer and wine. *Torula*, a species of yeast, is the 'bio' in biological washing powders, used to digest stains on clothing.

Mycelium and Miracle Growth

Fungi can be divided into two sub-groups: the microfungi, including the moulds, yeasts and similar microscopic organisms; and the macrofungi, the familiar mushrooms and toadstools that are illustrated in this book. The structure of most fungi consists of a mycelium, a dense network of interconnecting threads that are known individually as hypha (plural: hyphae). The mycelium is the true body of the fungus but even in the macrofungi it is usually so small that it is invisible to the naked eye. When hyphae fuse, they produce the fruiting body of the fungus, also known as a carpophore or sporophore, which in the macrofungi is the mushroom or toadstool itself.

Sometimes, the hyphae clump together into long, thick filaments that look like bootlaces and are known as rhizomorphs; these are used mainly by parasitic macrofungi to attack the roots of a host plant. Two common parasitic species of macrofungi that create rhizomorphs are the Honey Fungus (p. 46) and the Whitelaced Shank (p. 50).

Hyphae also play a crucial role in symbiotic mycorrhizal associations between fungi and plants (usually trees). In this relationship the hyphae intertwine with the roots of the plant, absorbing food from the plant and in return supplying it with minerals. Many forest-dwelling fungi are mycorrhizal species, including almost all of the boletes (pp. 16–23), and many trees cannot flourish without them. In fact, all of the green plants that fix nitrogen in the soil, such as clovers, do so because their roots are inhabited by microfungi.

Some fungal mycelia spread over huge distances. A good example is the Fairy Ring Champignon (p. 59), whose mycelium radiates in a circle from a single spore. Mycelia, in fact, cover most of the Earth, forming a dense mat of branching and interconnecting hyphae, so that 1cu m of soil can contain as much as 7,850km of mycelium. The world's largest living organism in terms of area, which covered 8,900ha before it was dissected by logging roads, was found in a forest in the Blue Mountains of eastern Oregon, USA. It consisted of a single mycelium of *Armillaria ostoyae*, a type of honey fungus, estimated to be 2,200 years old. The species is both saprophytic and parasitic, living on trees and killing them, before colonising the next generation of trees that grows in their place.

FUNGAL DISTRIBUTION

Because spores weigh so little, they can be carried in the upper atmosphere, the result being that many members of the same species of fungus can be found in different parts of the world. The Fly Agaric (p. 36), for example, is found in all the temperate regions. Other fungi that were once confined to a small area have now spread far and wide. One example is the Cage Fungus *Clathrus cancellatus*, a gasteromycete native to Australasia that is now found in Europe as a result of raw wool fleeces containing the spores being imported from Australia. Fungi can grow on almost any substrate – wood, clothing, carpets, insects and animals (including humans), requiring simply warmth and humidity, especially the latter, as the fruiting body consists largely of water. Most macrofungi fruit on the ground in grassland and woodland, and on trees. A few species, known as hypogeous fungi, of which truffles are an example, spend their entire life cycle underground. Some large fungi grow on living or dead trees branches.

A few of the larger fungi produce their fruiting bodies in the spring, including the St George's Mushroom (p. 49) and the Morel (p. 151). By far the majority, however, appear from summer to autumn (August to October in Europe), with a few, such as Deer Shield (p. 72), surviving until the first winter frosts. Some of the tougher bracket fungi that grow on trees, such as the Hairy Curtain Crust (p. 107), survive the winter in a dormant state and grow year after year, adding more brackets or layers to existing brackets during their growing season.

Some fungi favour high ground, others lowland, while still others can grow at any altitude. Some fungi may be rare in some places and abundant in others; the same fungi will not necessarily be found in the same locality year after year. That is why I have deliberately refrained from referring to the rarity or otherwise of particular species in this book. To quote John Bingham in his 2008 report 'Fungal Changes in Worcestershire' (www.wbrc.org.uk): 'Fungi are not like insects that spread north in response to a warmer climate. Or like plants that tend appear at a point source and spread steadily outwards along roads or railways. We don't really know what species we have in Worcestershire. New species may not be new just not recorded for years. Some fungi fruit only once in 30 or even 50 years and even then you need to at the right place at the right time – a matter of a few days to catch many fruiting? Even if you can name a fungus the name will have changed from older records – so it may not be obvious.'

STRUCTURE OF THE LARGER FUNGI

Fungi are classified by the manner in which they carry their spores. Most of the macrofungi fall into the category of basidiomycetes, or club fungi, characterised by having a basidium, a club-shaped structure on which the spores are carried. There are usually four spores on each basidium, although sometimes they number only two. A much smaller number of the macrofungi fall into another category, one that contains far more microscopic fungi, namely the ascomycetes. These fungi hold their spores in an ascus, or sac; examples in this book are the morels (pp. 151–2).

THE BASIDIOMYCETES

By far the most familiar of the basidiomycetes are the agarics, or gill fungi. The best known is the Cultivated Mushroom *Agaricus bisporus*. In gill fungi, the fruiting body starts to grow when hyphae from the mycelium coalesce to form a small lump in the shape of an egg. Inside this 'egg', known as the universal veil, the fruiting body forms, bursting out in the shape of a button mushroom that then grows rapidly to maturity. The spores are grouped in twos or fours on the club-shaped basidia attached to the gills, and when mature they fall off the little stalk attaching them to the basidium and disperse.

The agarics are divided into sub-families based on their structure, whether or not they have a volva (a sheath around the base of the stem, the remains of the 'egg' from which they grew), a ring (some fungi have a protective veil over the gills when young; this later breaks away to form a ring or it may leave fragments on the cap) or both. Another clue to identifying a species of gill fungus is the way in which the gills are attached to the cap and stem. There are five basic patterns: adnate, in which the gills are attached to the stem but do not run down it; adnexed, where they are only partially attached to the stem; sub-decurrent, where they run down the stem a little way; decurrent, where they run down the stem quite a long way (typical of the funnel caps); and free, where they are not attached to the stem at all (a classic example of this type is the Parasol (p. 33). Gills may also be sinuate, being notched near their point of attachment to the stem, they may be crowded (dense) or widely spaced, and they may or may not fork or be of uneven lengths.

CHECKING SPORE COLOUR

Spore colour is also used to identify gill fungi. The way the spores of a gill fungus can be seen without a microscope is to make a spore print of them. To do this, cut off the cap of a mature mushroom just under the stem and place it on a sheet of pale blue paper (this

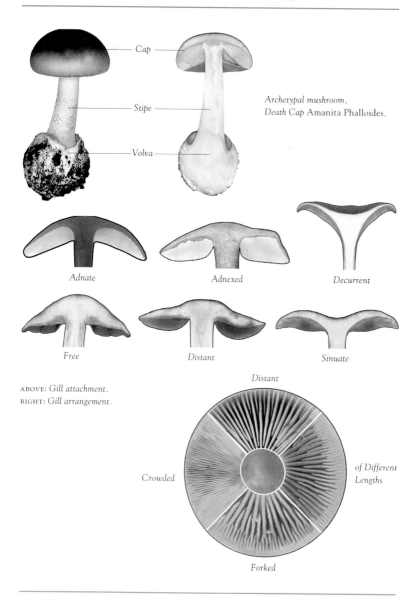

Cap

Stipe

Volva

Archetypal mushroom,
Death Cap Amanita Phalloides.

Adnate

Adnexed

Decurrent

Free

Distant

Sinuate

ABOVE: *Gill attachment.*
RIGHT: *Gill arrangement.*

Distant

Crowded

*of Different
Lengths*

Forked

A spore print from a cultivated mushroom (Agaricus bisporus), and on the right the cap from which it was produced.

is the best colour, as there are no blue spores, so even if the spores are white they can be clearly seen). Leave the cap on the paper in a spot where there are no drafts (such as inside a microwave oven or under a wide-mouthed jar) for 24 hours, then remove the cap. You should have a print showing the colour of the spores, arranged neatly in the pattern of the gills.

OTHER BASIDIOMYCETES

Not all basidiomycetes have gills, as there are many ways in which the spores are carried. The boletes are shaped like the classic mushroom, but instead of gills they have tightly packed tubes ending in pores, from which the spores emerge. The hedgehog mushrooms, such as the Wood Hedgehog (p. 143), have tiny spines in place of the gills. Then there are the gasteromycetes, fungi that carry their spores on a glebum, a spore-carrying layer of membrane, such as the stinkhorns (p. 114), puffballs (pp. 128–31) and earthballs (p. 132).

The club fungi are club-shaped or branching like the antlers of a deer (pp. 108–11), and the bird's nest fungi (pp. 127–8) produce spores in egg-shaped structures called peridioles.

THE ASCOMYCETES

Most ascomycetes are microfungi, but there are a few larger fungi that also fall into this category. All are easy to recognise. They include the morels (pp. 151–2), the Summer Truffle *Tuber aestivum*, which grows in temperate regions, the Périgord or Black Truffle *T. melanosporum* and the White Truffle *T. magnatum*. The last two species are among the most expensive foods in the world; they are found only in southern Europe. Truffles are hypogeous, meaning that they spend their life cycle underground.

NOMENCLATURE

Like all living things, species of fungi have a binomial scientific name consisting of a genus name and a species epithet, following a system devised by Swedish scientist Carl Linnaeus in the 18th century. The practice and science of classifying species in this way is known as taxonomy, and the name applied to a taxonomic group in a formal system of nomenclature is a taxon (plural: taxa). In scientific works, the genus name and species epithet are followed by the abbreviated or full name of the scientist who first classified the species, for example, *Agaricus campestris* L., showing that it was Linnaeus himself who first gave the Field Mushroom its name. When a species is reclassified, the former scientist's name appears in brackets, followed by the name of the scientist who renamed it, as in *Lactarius deliciosus* (L.) Gray. The scientific name for a species is the same throughout the world, unlike the common name, which varies from country to country and language to language, or may be one of several used to refer to the same fungus.

Unfortunately, many species of fungi have been reclassified several times and hence have undergone numerous name changes, so that older field guides give different scientific names to those found in modern books or the authorities cannot agree on the same scientific name. For this reason, each species listed in this book appears with its current scientific name and any names by which it is also or has recently been known. As for common names, until recently only the most familiar fungi, such as the Cep (p. 16), the Fly Agaric (p. 36) and the Chanterelle (p. 103), had these, but many of the macrofungi have now been given English names by authorities such as the Royal Botanic Gardens at Kew or the British Mycological Society (BMS). The BMS has a committee to decide on the official common name of each species, and these have mostly been used in this guide.

Some relatively common fungi continue to be known exclusively by their scientific name. For this reason and to be certain of identification, it is important to remember the species by these names. This will allow you to identify them to other mycologists anywhere in the world, even if you do not speak the same language.

MUSHROOM HUNTING

When hunting for mushrooms, use a flat-bottomed basket such as a trug. Separate the mushrooms in small paper bags, never plastic bags, as the lack of air and the closed atmosphere will cause them to deteriorate. A short, sharp knife (special mushrooming knives are available) is useful for scraping off leaf mould and other debris, but try not to cut off the stem as it can be important for identification purposes. A magnifying glass or hand lens is useful in the field, and at home a microscope will show you the fungus structure in a detail invisible to the naked eye.

SAFETY FIRST

Unfortunately, one of the problems in identifying gill fungi is that they can vary considerably in appearance, depending on the substrate on which they grow, the weather conditions and the nutrients they are absorbing from the soil. That is why it is essential, even for the seasoned mushroom hunter, to eat only those mushrooms that can be identified with certainty. It is advisable for the beginner to avoid all-white mushrooms, for instance, as poisonous species can easily be confused with those that are edible. Always keep the different species separate when you collect them, as spores from a poisonous mushroom could contaminate the edible ones.

For identification purposes, it is advisable to use more than one field guide. Some illustrations and photographs can make a particular species look very different from how it appears in the field, and not every species is described in every book. Even though fungi do not move about, they are very hard to photograph *in situ*, as their important features tend to be hidden by leaves, earth, grass, and so on. That is why a coloured illustration of a fungus can be just as reliable as a photograph for identification purposes. Always use reputable field guides, not the Internet (with the exception of the BMA's website; see p. 156), for identification purposes, as many of the descriptions on unofficial sites are inaccurate. When photographing fungi yourself, you will need a camera fitted with a macro lens.

EATING MUSHROOMS SAFELY

It is probably a truism to write that there are no general rules about fungus edibility, and that each species must be assessed on its own merits. Stories that mushrooms are edible if the cap can be peeled away or if a silver spoon does not turn black when cooked with them are dangerous fictions. Certain fungi have haemolytic properties (they destroy red blood cells) when raw and so should not be eaten in that state, while others – especially the Common Inkcap (p. 96) – cause a bad reaction when consumed with alcohol, or even if you have a drink up to three days after eating them. Poisonous fungi contain different types of toxins that react in different ways. They may be merely indigestible, such as the Yellow Stainer (see p. 91), and cause no long-lasting damage, but others may be deadly, such as the amanitas (pp. 36–40), the pinkgills (p. 71) and the Brown Rollrim (p. 79). The edibility of the species listed in this guide is given at the end of each description.

Even wild mushrooms that are supposed to be perfectly edible should be treated with caution. Mushrooms decay in the same way as meat, so they should not be eaten when in a deteriorated state or if they are waterlogged, as this can conceal decay. Never eat a mushroom that has been parasitised by another fungus, and do not eat mushrooms from soil that is liable to be polluted. Fungi are the most efficient absorbers of pollutants such as heavy metals and radiation, but the down side of this is that they can be safely eaten only if they are growing in unpolluted areas. Do not eat any that are growing next to main roads or close to other sources of pollution or radiation. Clean all mushrooms carefully (you can use a special mushroom-cleaning brush for this) and eat them as soon as possible after picking.

NUTRITIONAL VALUE

Fungi were once thought to have little nutritional value, but it is now realised that they contain protein and are the only non-animal source of vitamin B12, so they are particularly important in the diet of vegetarians and vegans. They also contain significant levels of trace elements, such as phosphorus, potassium and copper. The different varieties of the Cultivated Mushroom *Agaricus bisporus* and related species are high in nutrients.

I hope that this swift overview of the properties of fungi has given you some insight into this important but little-known area of the natural world and will encourage you to investigate it further.

Glossary

Adnate Where the gills or tubes are attached to the stem along their entire width.

Adnexed Where the gills or tubes are narrowly attached to the stem by less than their entire width.

Aethalium (pl. aethalia) Spore-bearing mass in the more primitive slime fungi (myxomycetes), equivalent to the fruiting body of a macrofungus.

Agaric Gill fungus.

Anastomosed Folds, and sometimes gills, that are forked and joined by veins, as in the rollrims.

Ascomycete Fungi of the phylum Ascomycota, in which the spores are held in sacs (asci).

Ascus The sac containing the spores of an ascomycete.

Basidiocarp The fruiting body containing the basidium; a synonym for carpophore or fruiting body, but applicable only to basidiomycetes.

Basidiomycete Fungi of the phylum Basidiomycota, whose spores are held on a club-shaped organ, the basidium, before they are released.

Basidium Club-shaped organ on which the spores are held in twos or fours.

Campanulate Bell-shaped; used to describe a cap, as in the Liberty Cap (p. 89).

Carpophore See 'Sporophore'.

Cespitose Growing in clumps, where the stem of each specimen is attached to that of its neighbour, as in the case of the scalycaps.

Chlamydospore A large, thick-walled spore enabling the fungus to survive for long periods in unfavourable conditions.

Conidiophore A simple or branched hypha of a fungus on which asexual spores (conidia) are borne.

Conidium (pl. conidia) An asexual spore.

Cortina Thin veil covering the edge of the cap and joined to the stem. As the mushroom grows, the veil tears, leaving fragments attached to the cap or a wispy ring on the stem, or both, as in the webcaps.

Cuticle Thin skin covering the cap. The flesh under the cuticle may be of a different colour, as in the Red-cracking Bolete (p. 18).

Decurrent Gills, tubes or spines that run down the stem.

Deliquescent Liquefying. Most species of inkcap deliquesce as they mature.

Depressed With a central or lateral depression, as in the funnel caps.

Detached Describes gills that are not attached to the stem.

Eccentric Off-centre.

Emarginate Describes gills that have a notch at the point of attachment to the stem. See also 'Marginate'. Also describes a smooth bulb without a ridge.

Endoperidium An internal membrane or sac encasing the fruiting bodies of certain fungi, especially puffballs and other gasteromycetes.

Exoperidium Skin or membrane covering the fruiting body of certain fungi, especially gasteromycetes such as the puffballs.

Fasciculate Growing in tight clumps that consist of many specimens, such as Sulphur Tuft (p. 85).

Fibrillose Covered in short fibres or hairs.
Floccose Covered in flakes, scales or thick down.
Foot The base of the stem.
Free Describing gills that touch the stem but are not attached to it.
Fruiting body See 'Sporophore'.
Fugacious Ephemeral; often used to describe a ring or cortina that disappears with age.
Funiculus The cord that attaches the peridioles to the peridium (the 'nest') in bird's nest fungi.
Gasteromycete Member of a group of fungi that bear their spores in an enclosed area, rather than on gills or tubes; examples are the puffballs and the bird's nest fungi.
Gleba Mass of spore-bearing tissue in fungi such as puffballs, earthballs and truffles.
Globose Spherical.
Granulose Covered in small granules or spots.
Hygrophanous Changing appearance and colour depending on the degree of humidity in the atmosphere, as in the case of the Sheathed Woodtuft (p. 85).
Hymenium The fertile part of the fruiting body.
Hypha (pl. hyphae) One of the mass of threads of which the fungus mycelium consists.
Hypogeous Having a subterranean fruiting body, as in the truffles.
Imbricated Piled on top of each other in tiers, as in Oyster Mushroom caps (p. 99).
Irregular Describes gills of different lengths.
Macrofungus A large mushroom or toadstool, easily visible to the naked eye.
Margin The edge of the cap.
Marginate Describes a bulb with a clearly marked edge or ridge. Smoothly rounded bulbs are said to be emarginate.
Microfungus A fungus whose details cannot be seen with the naked eye, such as a mould.
Mycelium Network of underground filaments, or hyphae, that are the actual vegetative part of the fungus.
Mycology The branch of natural history devoted to the study of fungi.
Mycorrhiza A symbiotic association between the mycelium of a fungus and the roots of plants, especially trees. See also 'Symbiosis'.
Myxomycete A slime mould consisting of a shapeless mass, the plasmodium, that is capable of moving over the substrate. They used to be classified as fungi, but are now considered separate organisms.
Ostiole Small orifice through which the spores of certain species, such as the puffballs, can escape into the air.
Ozonium A thick, shaggy carpet of mycelium produced by certain macrofungi, especially the Firerug Inkcap (p. 97).
Partial veil Envelope that protects the hymenium of certain young mushrooms. It may persist in the form of a ring.
Peridiole The 'egg' containing the basidiospores in bird's nest fungi.
Peridium Membrane enveloping fungi such as the puffballs, earthballs and truffles. It consists of two layers, the exoperidium and the endoperidium.

Perithecium (pl. perithecia) The flask- or cup-shaped fruiting body of the birds' nest fungi, or the sexual fruiting body in the Coral Spot fungus (p. 151).

Persistent Usually used to refer to a ring, meaning that it does not disappear with age.

Pileus Another name for the cap.

Resupinate Fungi that form a crust on the substrate on which they grow.

Reticulate Having a net-like covering, like the netting that covers the stem of certain boletes.

Rhizomorph A root-like extension of the mycelium that entwines around the host.

Saprophyte An organism that feeds off dead plants.

Sclerotium A minute accumulation of hyphae, usually black, produced by parasitic fungi when the host disappears, and which enables them to survive until the next host is found.

Sessile Lacking a stem, as in the case of certain polypores.

Seta (pl. setae) A tiny bristle.

Sinuate Wavy. Used to describe gills that have a sudden curve near the stem.

Slime mould See 'Myxomycete'.

Spatulate In the shape of a spade or spatula.

Spore Microscopic reproductive structure of all fungi.

Sporophore The fruit or fruiting body produced by the fungus, containing the spores by which the fungus reproduces. In the gill fungi, the sporophore is the mushroom or toadstool. Also known as the carpophore.

Squamule A tiny scale or hairy tuft.

Stipe Another name for the stem.

Striated Marked with grooves, often at the margin of gill fungi.

Sub-decurrent Where the gills do not run entirely down the stem but are attached along more of the stem than adnate gills.

Symbiosis In the case of mushrooms, used to describe the mycorrhizal association between a fungus and a higher form of vegetation, usually a tree. See also 'Mycorrhiza'.

Umbilicate Describes a cap that has a central depression like a navel.

Umbo The central knob in the cap of some species.

Umbonate Describes a cap with an umbo surrounded by a shallow trough, as in the Trumpet Chanterelle (p. 104).

Universal veil Membrane covering a young specimen that may persist into maturity in the form of scales or patches on the cap, plus a volva at the base of the stem.

Vesicle A small sac enclosed in a membrane that stores or transports substances in a liquid.

Volva Cup-shaped remnant of the universal veil, covering the base of the stem in certain species of gill fungi.

Zoned A cap covered in concentric circles, such as in the Saffron Milkcap (p. 25).

Cep ■ *Boletus edulis*
Cap 6–25cm, height 6–25cm

SYNONYMS Penny Bun, Porcini.
DESCRIPTION In all boletes, the underside of the cap consists of pores, not gills. These are the ends of densely packed tubes that are easily separable from the flesh of the cap. The cap of the Cep is sepia-brown and the pores start white and age to yellow. Unlike many other boletes, the flesh never changes colour. The most distinguishing feature of the Cep is its swollen stem, which is often wider than the cap and covered in white reticulation. The cap is shiny in dry weather, slightly sticky in damp weather.
HABITAT On the ground in deciduous woods, especially oak, but also found among conifers. Jul–Nov.
POSSIBLE CONFUSION Bay Bolete (p. 18).
EDIBILITY Edible and delicious. One of the few wild mushrooms easily available commercially, usually in dried form.

Rooting Bolete ■ *Boletus radicans*
Cap 20cm, height 5–15cm

SYNONYM Whitish Bolete.
DESCRIPTION Large summer bolete, recognisable by its dry velvety cap, which varies in colour from beige to pale grey; it has a strongly inrolled margin when young. The pores are lemon-yellow and the flesh is white or bluish white; both pores and flesh turn blue when bruised or cut. The stem, which broadens towards the swollen foot, is white with yellow reticulation just under the cap, and is sometimes streaked with red. The foot usually has a pointed tip, and its upper part is sometimes streaked with red. The flesh has an unpleasant smell and bitter taste.
HABITAT Deciduous trees on both limestone and acid soil. Late summer to autumn.
EDIBILITY Not edible.

Scarletina Bolete

■ *Boletus luridiformis*
Cap 6–20cm, height 6–20cm

SYNONYMS Red-stalked Bolete,
B. *erythropus*.
DESCRIPTION The brownish-olive
cap contains thick yellow flesh that
turns indigo when bruised. The
smell and taste are pleasant. The
pores are small, yellow at first and
turning deep red with age. The stem
is densely red-dotted.
HABITAT On the ground, usually
in deciduous woods. Late summer to
autumn
EDIBILITY Edible, but should not be
eaten raw or with alcohol.

Devil's Bolete

■ *Boletus satanas*
Cap 10–25cm, height 6–10cm

DESCRIPTION This handsome,
distinctive bolete has been classified
as an endangered species in the UK.
The thick, fleshy cap is off-white
and dome-shaped, with an irregular
margin. The flesh is white or pale
yellow. The pores are vivid red. The
short, thick stem is yellow under
the cap, sometimes covered in red
reticulation, bright red in the middle
and white at the base. The smell
is faint when young, unpleasant in
older specimens.
HABITAT In clearings in deciduous
woods (especially Beech *Fagus
sylvatica*, on calcareous soil, and oak)

and beside paths. Summer and autumn, preferring warm weather.
EDIBILITY **Poisonous**. All red-pored boletes are believed to be toxic.

Boletus cisalpinus
Cap 4–11cm, height 5–13cm

SYNONYM *Xerocomus cisalpinus*.

DESCRIPTION The cap varies in colour from beige to dark brown, depending on the weather, and is smooth when young but soon begins to crack all over, showing pink underneath. The stem is usually subtly two-toned, grading from reddish at the base to reddish yellow above. The flesh is red only where it shows under the cap, otherwise it is yellow and soft. The pores are yellow, turning olive with age. The flesh, stem and pores turn blue when cut or bruised.

HABITAT Under broadleaved trees, especially oaks and beech.

POSSIBLE CONFUSION Resembles 3 other species in which the cap also cracks: Suede Bolete (p. 20), Red-cracking Bolete *B. chrysenteron* and White-cracking Bolete *B. porosporus*.

EDIBILITY Edible.

Bay Bolete
■ *Boletus badius*
Cap 5–15cm, height 5–15cm

SYNONYM *Xerocomus badius*.

DESCRIPTION The dark brown cap is velvety when dry but slimy when wet, rounded and convex, and sometimes irregular. The pores are whitish in young specimens, later turning yellow, and finally olive-green. The pale yellow flesh, which turns faintly blue when cut, has a mild flavour and odour. The stem may be thick or thin, but it is always covered in red or reddish-brown streaks on a yellow ground, except directly under the cap, where it is pale yellow.

HABITAT On the ground, often under spruce and pine, less frequently under Beech *Fagus sylvatica* and oak trees. Autumn.

POSSIBLE CONFUSION Looks a little like the Cep (p. 16), but its cap is darker and the stem is slimmer. May also be confused with Suede Bolete (p. 20).

EDIBILITY Edible.

Ruby Bolete

■ *Boletus rubellus*
Cap 4–8cm, height 4–8cm

SYNONYMS B. *versicolor*,
Xerocomus rubellus, X. versicolor.
DESCRIPTION Fairly distinctive,
as it is the only red-stemmed bolete
with a bright red cap. The cap is
velvety when dry but slimy when
wet, rounded and convex. The
pores and tubes are pale yellow in
young specimens, turning yellow,
and finally olive-green. The flesh is
pale yellow and the stem is bright
yellow, streaked with red. The base
of the stem is slightly swollen. The
smell and taste are pleasant.
HABITAT In open, deciduous
woodland; usually associated with
oaks. Autumn.
EDIBILITY Not edible.

Matt Bolete

■ *Boletus pruinatus*
Cap 5–10cm, height 5–10cm

SYNONYMS Downy Bolete,
Xerocomus pruinatus.
DESCRIPTION The velvety cap,
covered in a whitish down when
dry, is pale brown to olive in colour.
It is hemispherical when young,
flattening in older specimens. The
flesh is lemon yellow. The pores
are pale to bright yellow, and do
not darken with age. The stem is
a bright, uniform yellow and turns
blue when damaged.
HABITAT Mainly under Beech
Fagus sylvatica. Summer and
autumn.
EDIBILITY Edible but not good.

Suede Bolete

▪ *Boletus subtomentosus*
Cap 5–12cm, height <8cm

SYNONYM *Xerocomus subtomentosus*.
DESCRIPTION Domed, light brown
cap, the texture of suede. The flesh is
pale yellow and does not change colour
when cut or bruised. The stem is often
curved, thickening at the base and
streaked with reddish brown. The bright
yellow pores are wide, especially near
the stem, and are irregular and angular.
The taste and smell are pleasant.
HABITAT Under deciduous and
coniferous trees, often in the company
of Red-cracking Bolete (p. 18). Does
not like limestone soil. Summer and
autumn.
POSSIBLE CONFUSION Easily confused
with atypical specimens of the Red-cracking and Bay boletes (p. 18).
EDIBILITY Edible but not good.

Orange Birch Bolete

▪ *Leccinum versipelle*
Cap 6–13cm, height 9–18cm

SYNONYMS *Boletus versipellis,
B. testaceo-scaber, L. testaceo-scabrum*.
DESCRIPTION The *Leccinum* boletes
have a white stem, covered in tufts of
a darker colour, and a dry, convex cap.
The Orange Birch Bolete has an orange
cap that extends in a fringe beyond the
pores; this, and its distinctive colouring,
make identification easy. The flesh is
white, turning greyish when old, and
turning blue-green at the base of the
stem. The pores are tiny and whitish,
eventually turning grey. The stem is covered in tiny black scales on a white background,
and bulges in the middle.
HABITAT Always under birch trees, mainly in clearings and on heathland. Summer and
autumn.
EDIBILITY Edible.

Orange Oak Bolete

■ *Leccinum aurantiacum*
Cap 10–20cm, height 6–15cm

SYNONYM *L. quercinum*, *Boletus aurantiacus*.

DESCRIPTION The bright orange cap is dome-shaped at first and quite small, barely wider than the stem, eventually spreading until almost flat. The velvety cuticle overlaps the margin. The flesh is thick, whitish and firm in the stem, darkening to pinkish grey when cut, and darkening further when cooked, as in all the *Leccinum* species. The smell and taste are pleasant. The pores are small and white, turning grey-brown with age. The stem is white but thickly covered with small reddish-brown tufts.

HABITAT On the ground in association with birches, Hornbeam *Carpinus betulus*, Aspen *Populus tremula* and poplars. Prefers damp clay soil. Summer and autumn.

EDIBILITY Edible when young.

Brown Birch Bolete

■ *Leccinum scabrum*
Cap 5–10cm, height 8–12cm

SYNONYMS Rough Bolete, *Boletus scaber*.

DESCRIPTION The cap is dry, hemispherical at first and then flattening to slightly convex. It is grey-brown. The flesh is white and does not change colour when cut. It has a mild, pleasant smell. The long stem is white and fibrous, narrowing at the top and covered in greyish-black scales. The pores are white, turning grey with age and darkening to the touch.

HABITAT Grows under birches, even when they are mixed with other trees, on damp acid soil. Summer to autumn.

POSSIBLE CONFUSION Mottled Bolete *Leccinum variicolor* is similar and also grows under birches.

EDIBILITY Edible but not good.

Slippery Jack ▪ *Suillus luteus*
Cap 5–12cm, height 7–13cm

SYNONYMS *Boletus luteus*.

DESCRIPTION The genus *Suillus* contains boletes whose caps are always slimy and that have a veil covering the pores in the young stage, this later tearing to form a ring around the stem. Slippery Jack is probably the best known of the group. It has a large, thick, fleshy cap whose cuticle is generally chestnut-brown but may be paler. The cap is coated in a thick slime, to which pine needles and other debris stick, especially in wet weather. Sometimes fragments of the veil cling to the margin of the cap. The ring is white in young specimens but later darkens to greyish purple. The pores and tubes are yellow, darkening to ochre with age. The flesh is white to yellowish and does not change colour. The stem is cylindrical, thick and firm, yellow above the ring and whitish below it, and covered with small red spots.

HABITAT In clumps under pine trees, especially on high ground. Occasionally found in spring but mainly in autumn.

EDIBILITY Edible.

Larch Bolete
▪ *Suillus grevillei* Cap 5–10cm, height 6–16cm

SYNONYMS Elegant Bolete, *Boletus grevillei, B. elegans*.

DESCRIPTION Easy to recognise because it is a uniform yellow, varying in shade from daffodil to light brown. In young specimens, the cap may be pale brown. The veil and later the ring are white and fluffy. The flesh is pale yellow under the cap and bright yellow in the stem. The pores turn brown when bruised and with age, and sometimes exude slimy droplets. The surface of the stem below the ring is covered with red veins or spots that vary from very marked to barely visible.

HABITAT Exclusively under larches. Jul–Oct.

EDIBILITY Edible.

Bovine Bolete ■ *Suillus bovinus*
Cap 5–10cm, height 4–10cm

SYNONYM *Boletus bovinus*.
DESCRIPTION The cap is shiny and viscous when damp, convex at first, then flattening almost completely in mature specimens, with a slight central mound. The cap flesh is thick in the centre, soft and elastic, and yellowish white. The tubes are angular and composite (divided into compartments), and end in wide pores; they are difficult to separate from one another (a distinctive feature). The pores are beige at first, darkening to greenish yellow. The stem is slender and flexible, becoming covered in red fibres as it ages.
HABITAT Found only under pines, often growing in clumps on heathland, in acid soil at all altitudes. Often found in the company of the gill fungus Rosy Spike (p. 102). Late summer to autumn.
EDIBILITY Edible but not good.

Parasitic Bolete
■ *Pseudoboletus parasiticus*
Cap 3–5cm, height 6–8cm

SYNONYMS *Boletus parasiticus*, *Xerocomus parasiticus*.
DESCRIPTION One of the very few macrofungi that is parasitic on other fungi, and 1 of only 2 known parasitic boletes in the world. The cap is convex, then flat, dry and slightly downy, and olive-brown in colour. The stem is usually curved and slender, and yellow with rusty streaks. The flesh is yellowish and does not change colour when cut.
HABITAT Parasitises the Common Earthball (p. 132), usually growing in clusters around the fruiting body of the host as it

attacks the mycelium below ground. On heathland on sandy soil. Autumn.
EDIBILITY Edible but not good.

Peppery Milkcap

■ *Lactarius piperatus*
Cap 10–16cm, height 6–8cm

DESCRIPTION Milkcaps are gill fungi like the agaric mushroom, but their unmistakable feature is that they exude a milky liquid if the gills are cut or bruised. The cap is often funnel-shaped or has a depressed centre when mature, and the gills are often decurrent. In the Peppery Milkcap, the stem, densely crowded gills, milk and spores are all white. The milk is plentiful and has a strong peppery flavour. The cap is smooth and shiny in wet weather; the margin remains inrolled until old, becoming deeply funnel-shaped in mature specimens.

HABITAT On the ground in damp places in deciduous woods. Autumn.

EDIBILITY Edible but not recommended. Eaten only in eastern Europe, where the flesh is used as a substitute for pepper.

Woolly Milkcap

■ *Lactarius torminosus*
Cap 4–9cm, height 6–8cm

DESCRIPTION Recognisable by its pink colour and shaggy cap, whose margin is deeply inrolled in younger specimens. The cap, slightly depressed in mature fungi, is pale pink, banded with rings of darker pink. The milk is white and very peppery. The crowded gills are cream or pink. The thick stem is the same colour as the gills and is sometimes pitted.

HABITAT Mainly under birches, but also under conifers at high altitude. Prefers open ground. Summer and autumn.

POSSIBLE CONFUSION Bearded Milkcap *L. pubescens* is similar but less hairy, smaller and paler. The Saffron Milkcap (p. 25) is also similar but the milk is quite different in colour.

EDIBILITY Not edible. Bitter and indigestible.

Yellowdrop Milkcap

■ *Lactarius chrysorrheus*
Cap 4–8cm, height 4–9cm

DESCRIPTION The name of this milkcap reveals its most obvious characteristic – its abundant milk, which is white at first but soon turns sulphur-yellow when exposed to the air. The pale pinkish-orange cap, lightly marked with darker concentric rings, is slightly depressed in the centre and the margin is inrolled at first. The gills are crowded and cream-coloured. The white flesh turns bright yellow when broken.

HABITAT Grows in deciduous woods, mainly under oaks, Beech *Fagus sylvatica* and Sweet Chestnut *Castanea sativa*. Late summer to autumn.

POSSIBLE CONFUSION The only other milkcap that exudes yellow milk is the Deceiving Milkcap *L. decipiens*, but its cap is uniformly red and it smells strongly of geraniums.

EDIBILITY Not edible. Bitter and indigestible.

Saffron Milkcap

■ *Lactarius deliciosus*
Cap 5–12cm, height 4–8cm

The cap is inrolled at first, wavy or flattened, and eventually depressed in the centre. It is pale orange with concentric rings of darker orange, gaining green patches with age. The pinkish-orange gills are tightly packed and sub-decurrent, spotting green with age like the cap. The flesh is pale yellow to orange, thick and firm. The milk is bright orange, turning greenish upon exposure to air. The smell is fruity and the taste slightly spicy.

HABITAT Found exclusively under conifers, especially pines. Prefers limestone or sandy soils. Has a long summer and autumn growing season.

POSSIBLE CONFUSION The False Saffron Milkcap *L. deterrimus*, once considered a variety of the Saffron Milkcap, grows under spruces. It turns green more quickly and is inedible. May also be confused with Woolly Milkcap (p. 24).

EDIBILITY Edible and delicious.

Beech Milkcap

■ *Lactarius blennius*
Cap 4–12cm, height 4–12cm

SYNONYM Slimy Milkcap.
This rather unprepossessing
species has white milk that turns
greyish green as it dries. The cap is
greyish brown, dotted with small,
round or oval patches of darker
brown that are often arranged
concentrically around the margin.
The gills are white but turn grey
when bruised. The spores are
cream to pale yellow. The stem is
also slimy, and is similar in colour
to the cap but paler.

HABITAT Grows only under Beech *Fagus sylvatica*. Summer and autumn.
POSSIBLE CONFUSION The similar *L. fluens* has a less viscid cap and a paler margin.
Found in deciduous woodland, usually under beech.
EDIBILITY Inedible.

Oakbug Milkcap

■ *Lactarius quietus*
Cap 5–6.5cm, height 7–9cm

SYNONYMS Oak Milkcap,
Southern Milkcap.
DESCRIPTION Tends to be very
variable. The cap is slightly
funnel-shaped and varies
considerably in colour from
greyish brown to *café au lait*, with
faintly darker zoning that tends
to disappear in mature specimens.
The decurrent gills and stem are
flesh-coloured or pale ochre. The
flesh and milk are white with a
characteristic oily smell, and do
not change colour when cut or
bruised. The stem is white but is
coloured at the base. The spores are pale pink.
HABITAT On acid soil under oaks. Late summer and autumn.
EDIBILITY Not edible.

Ugly Milkcap ■ *Lactarius turpis*
Cap 8–20cm, height 5–7cm

SYNONYMS Ugly One, *L. plumbeus*, *L. necator*.
DESCRIPTION The black to olive-brown colour
and irregular shape of the cap of this milkcap are
indeed unattractive but easily recognisable. The
cap is funnel-shaped, with a depressed centre in
older specimens. The cuticle is sticky when wet,
with an inrolled, smooth, felty margin. The gills
are decurrent, dirty white, turning brown when
damaged or with age. The milk is white, plentiful
and peppery. The short, fat stem is grey, often
heavily pitted.
HABITAT Grows only in association with birches,
in well-lit areas on heathland and common land.
Often hard to spot when deeply embedded in
grass. Autumn.

POSSIBLE CONFUSION Blackening Brittlegill (p. 28) is similar but does not exude milk.
EDIBILITY Not edible.

Grey Milkcap

■ *Lactarius vietus*
Cap 4–7cm, height 5–7cm

DESCRIPTION The cap, which
is slimy when moist, is pale
greyish brown. It is shallowly
convex when young, and as it
matures it flattens, becoming
slightly depressed in the centre.
The margin is wavy and paler
than the centre. The long stem
is paler than the cap, tall and
narrow, sometimes thickening
at the base. The gills are cream
and become greyer with age.
The milk is white, darkening
to pale grey when exposed to
the air. The flesh and milk taste
acrid.
HABITAT Sometimes grows in

large numbers, especially in bogs; associated with birch trees. Aug–Nov.
EDIBILITY Not edible.

Blackening Brittlegill ■ *Russula nigricans* Cap 7–20cm, height 4–9cm

DESCRIPTION The russulas are related to the milkcaps, having the same brittle, chalky flesh, but their gills do not exude milk. The cap of the Blackening Brittlegill is convex and

very inrolled when young. The gills are widely spaced, thick and of uneven length. They are white, turn red when bruised and eventually blacken with age. The flesh and the sturdy stem are white, then blacken with age. The flesh reddens on exposure to air. The smell is faint, but acrid in the gills. HABITAT Under deciduous and coniferous trees at all altitudes. Summer and autumn. POSSIBLE CONFUSION Looks like the Ugly Milkcap (p. 27) but does not exude milk. EDIBILITY Not edible.

Ochre Brittlegill ■ *Russula ochroleuca* Cap 5–10cm, height 5–8cm

DESCRIPTION Has an ochre or dark yellow cap; the gills and stem are white. The cap is convex and dome-shaped when young, flattening with a slight depression in the centre

and always unevenly shaped. The gills are crowded, sinuate and white at first, pale yellow in older specimens. The flesh is yellow under the cuticle, otherwise white and very friable. It is virtually odourless. The stem is thick, as in all russulas. HABITAT Grows under deciduous and coniferous trees at all altitudes. Summer and autumn. POSSIBLE CONFUSION Looks much like the Geranium Russula *R. fellea*, but that species has pale yellow gills and stem, and a strong geranium smell. EDIBILITY Not edible.

Yellow Swamp Brittlegill ■ *Russula claroflava* Cap 5–12cm, height 5–9cm

DESCRIPTION Has a bright egg-yellow cap, which is dome-shaped at first, then flattening and with a deep central depression. It is always regular in shape. Due to the stickiness of the cap, it is often concealed by the leaves and twigs that adhere to it. The gills are widely

spaced, ochre at first and greying with age. The flesh is white, turning grey when cut or bruised. The stem is thick and very white, occasionally striped with grey and greying with age.

HABITAT Under birches and Aspen *Populus tremulus*; often found in *Sphagnum* bogs. Summer and autumn.

POSSIBLE CONFUSION Easily confused with other yellow-capped brittlegills.

EDIBILITY Edible, but not recommended owing to the difficulty of positive identification.

The Sickener ■ *Russula emetica*
Cap 3–8cm, height 6–10cm

DESCRIPTION Has a bright red cap, veering to orange when old. It is inrolled at first, then flattening, with a wide central depression and furrowed margin. The cuticle peels away easily from the friable, pale pink or white flesh. The gills are crowded and white. The flesh of the cap and stem are white, tasting very acrid and bitter (tasting is not recommended). The stem is thick, slightly club-shaped and white.

HABITAT This and related species are found under conifers, often in *Sphagnum* bogs. Summer and autumn.

POSSIBLE CONFUSION There are several closely related red-capped species or subspecies of The Sickener.

EDIBILITY **Poisonous**, causing diarrhoea and vomiting, as its name implies.

Powdery Brittlegill
■ *Russula parazurea*
Cap 4–8cm, height 5–9cm

DESCRIPTION The cap varies in colour from blue-grey to brownish violet and appears to be covered in a thick white down or powder when dry, although this feature is not as noticeable in wet weather. The cap is dome-shaped when young, with a wide depression in the centre when mature. The cuticle peels away easily from the friable white flesh. The gills are crowded and white, turning creamy orange. The flesh of the cap and the thick stem are white and odourless. The flavour is mild, though slightly stronger in the gills.
HABITAT Grows in association with deciduous trees, mostly in open spaces. Summer and early autumn.
EDIBILITY Edible but not recommended.

Charcoal Burner
■ *Russula cyanoxantha*
Cap 5–15cm, height 6–11cm

DESCRIPTION The cap varies considerably in colour, often containing patches of different hues, but almost always including purplish black, hence its common name. It can also be brownish, grey or even greenish. The cap is dome-shaped when young, later flattening and becoming slightly depressed in the centre. The margin is regular, occasionally slightly wrinkled. The gills are narrow and crowded, white and waxy. The flesh of the cap and stem is white, pinkish under the cuticle. The flavour is mild, sometimes tasting of hazelnut. The thick stem is white, often narrowing towards the base.
HABITAT Found in association with oak, Beech *Fagus sylvatica* and birch trees, often growing in large numbers. Summer and early autumn.
EDIBILITY Edible and good; sold in German markets.

Birch Brittlegill
■ *Russula betularum*
Cap 2–5cm, height 6–11cm

DESCRIPTION This is one of the smaller russulas. The cap is convex, varying in colour from whitish to pale pink, turning ochre in the centre when mature and often with a central depression. The margin is sometimes furrowed when the cap is fully expanded. The cuticle peels away easily to reveal white flesh that tastes peppery. The stem is relatively long. The gills are also white, serrated and widely spaced. The spores are white.
HABITAT Damp places; exclusively associated with birches. Summer and early autumn.
POSSIBLE CONFUSION Resembles the Fragile Brittlegill *R. fragilis*, whose cap is usually a darker pink.
EDIBILITY **Poisonous**. Considered to be a relative of The Sickener (p. 29).

Primrose Brittlegill
■ *Russula sardonia*
Cap 4–10cm, height 6–11cm

SYNONYM *R. drimeia*.
DESCRIPTION The cap is convex at first, then flattening, but with a small central umbo. It is violet, dark crimson or maroon, very occasionally ochraceous. The flesh of the cap is compact and very firm, white or pale yellow, and pink under the cuticle. The smell is deceptively mild, but the flesh tastes bitter and unpleasant. The stem is downy or powdery white, tinged with purple or lilac, although sometimes completely white.
HABITAT Found in large colonies under pines in sandy soil. Summer and early autumn.
POSSIBLE CONFUSION Often confused with the Fruity Brittlegill *R. queletii*, which it resembles, but that species smells of apples and grows under spruces on limestone soil.
EDIBILITY Not edible.

Beechwood Sickener
■ *Russula nobilis*
Cap 4–7cm, height 2–5cm

SYNONYM *R. mairei*.
DESCRIPTION The scarlet cap is matt and velvety when dry, and sticky when damp. It becomes discoloured with ochre patches as the fungus ages. The flesh is thick and white, smelling faintly of fruit when young and of honey when old, and yellows with age. The gills are crowded and whitish, with a blue-green sheen when young. The thick stem is white and firm, sometimes thickening at the base, and greying when old.
HABITAT Grows in association with Beech *Fagus sylvatica* and occasionally under oaks, on acid soils. Autumn.
EDIBILITY **Poisonous**. Causes diarrhoea and vomiting; this is another relative of The Sickener (p. 29).

Purple Brittlegill
■ *Russula atropurpurea*
Cap 4–10cm, height 6–7cm

SYNONYM *R. krombholzii*.
DESCRIPTION The shiny, fleshy cap is purplish black in colour, darkening to almost black in the centre, and viscous when wet. It is convex, then flattened, and slightly depressed in the centre with a wavy margin when mature. The crowded gills are white or cream. The cylindrical white stem is relatively short and sometimes splashed with ochre, turning grey with age. The flesh is whitish, tasting slightly acrid, and has a faintly fruity smell.
HABITAT Grows under deciduous trees, mainly oaks, and sometimes under pines in grassy clearings and beside paths. Summer and early autumn.
EDIBILITY Not edible.

Parasol ■ *Macrolepiota procera*
Cap 25–40cm, height 12–30cm

SYNONYM Parasol Mushroom, *Lepiota procera*.

DESCRIPTION The handsome Parasol is one of the largest European fungi. Species in the genus *Macrolepiota* have a veil covering the gills in the young stage, this then breaking to leave scales on the cap and a thick ring on the stem. The round cap of the young Parasol has a distinctive 'drumstick' appearance, which expands to become campanulate and, finally, flat. The colour of the cap and scales is brownish grey. The long stem is thin and woody, the lower part covered in brown scales; the double ring is thick and movable. The crowded gills are off-white.

HABITAT In groups of 2 or 3 on siliceous soil in grassland near woods. Jul–Oct.

EDIBILITY Edible and delicious.

Shaggy Parasol
■ *Chlorophyllum rhacodes*
Cap 5–15cm, height 12–20cm

SYNONYMS *Macrolepiota rhacodes*, *Lepiota rhacodes*.

DESCRIPTION The Shaggy Parasol is smaller than the Parasol (*above*). The cap is campanulate, never flattening completely. It is shaggy and cream-coloured, and covered in brown scales, with a small brown patch in the centre. The double ring is thick, and the scales and flesh redden when cut or bruised. The long stem is bulbous at the base.

HABITAT Mainly under conifers. Jul–Oct.

POSSIBLE CONFUSION A couple of similar species, *C. rhacodes* var. *bohemica* and *Macrolepiota venenata*, have been blamed for stomach upsets, but these grow only on nitrate-rich substrates such as dung heaps.

EDIBILITY Edible and delicious. Avoid if not found in woods.

Freckled Dapperling

■ *Lepiota aspera*
Cap 4–10cm, height 4–12cm

SYNONYMS *L. acutesquamosa*
var. *furcata*, Cystolepiota aspera,
Echinoderma asperum.
DESCRIPTION A large mushroom
whose white cap is thickly
covered in prominent brown,
warty scales. The cap is conical
to hemispherical, never flattening
even when old. The thick,
membranous veil breaks in older
specimens, leaving a floppy ring.
The thin, forked white or cream
gills leave a white spore print.
The thick flesh is white and smells
unpleasantly of rubber. The brown
stem is thick and squat.
HABITAT On humus-rich soils, including parks and forests; also grows among nettles.
Autumn.
EDIBILITY Not edible.

Stinking Dapperling

■ *Lepiota cristata* Cap 2–5cm, height 4–6cm

SYNONYMS Crested Lepiota, Stinking
Parasol.
DESCRIPTION Belongs to the group of little
dapperlings, none of which should be eaten as
they are either suspect or poisonous. The white
cap is covered with brown scales that disappear
at the margin and coalesce in the centre into
a brown patch. The cap is dome-shaped at
first but flattens to leave a slight central umbo
when mature. The widely spaced gills and the
spores are white. The thin ring may disappear
completely in old specimens. The stem is long
and woody, whitish above the ring and pinkish
brown below.
HABITAT In deciduous woodland, gardens and
tracksides. Autumn.
EDIBILITY **Poisonous**.

Earthy Powdercap

■ *Cystoderma amianthinum*
Cap 2–5cm, height 3–7cm

SYNONYMS Earthy Powder-cap,
Saffron Parasol.
DESCRIPTION The granulose,
saffron-coloured cap is easily
detachable from the stem, is
dome-shaped at first, but flattening
to leave a small central umbo. It
is dry and powdery, often with
a shaggy or fringed margin. The
stem is also saffron-coloured; it is
granular below the ring zone. The
flesh is white, turning yellowish,
and has an unpleasant mouldy
smell. The adnexed gills are
crowded and the spores are white. The thin ring may disappear completely in old specimens.
HABITAT In damp woods on moss and in heathland, under willows or among Bracken
Pteridium aquilinum, especially on acid soil. Summer and autumn.
EDIBILITY Not edible.

Powdercap Strangler

■ *Squamanita paradoxa*
Cap 2–5cm, height 2–4cm

SYNONYM *Cystoderma paradoxum*.
DESCRIPTION A very rare parasite of the
Earthy Powdercap (*see above*). It takes over
the host from the middle of the stem upwards
as if grafted on to it. The cap and upper part
of the stem are thickly covered in grey-brown
to reddish-brown scales. The gills and spores
are white, discoloring with age. The cap is
3cm across, convex, becoming flatter with
age. The upper stem is paler than the cap and
makes a clear division with the lower part of
the stem. The gills are widely spaced and of
varying lengths. The thick ring is persistent.
HABITAT In woods on acid soil. Summer and
autumn. The species is believed to be parasitic
on decaying fungi but this is not certain.
EDIBILITY Not edible.

Fly Agaric ■ *Amanita muscaria*
Cap 5–15cm, height 10–20cm

DESCRIPTION The red-and-white toadstool familiar from fairytale illustrations is so called because pieces of it were once soaked in milk to attract and kill flies. The volva leaves warty white patches on the bright red to orange cap (although they may wash away in wet weather), along with a ring, which is the remains of the veil. The cap is convex at first, later flattening. The flesh, stem, gills and spores are all white. The cylindrical, brittle stem is scaly below the frilly ring, ending in a scaly bulb. In the button stage the red cap is covered by the thick, scaly, universal veil. The flesh is bitter.
HABITAT Under birch trees, and occasionally under pines. Autumn.
EDIBILITY **Poisonous**.

The Blusher ■ *Amanita rubescens*
Cap 8–12cm, height 8–12cm

DESCRIPTION The colour of the cap varies from pinkish brown to darker brown, with white warts that tend to cluster at the centre and disappear with age. The cap is convex at first, later flattening slightly. The flesh, stem, gills and spores are all white. The cylindrical stem is pinkish brown below the floppy ring and ends in a bulb whose faintly perceptible scales are the remains of the volva. The flesh of the cap and stem turn pinkish red when cut or bruised, hence the species' common name.
HABITAT Under coniferous and deciduous trees. Summer to autumn.
POSSIBLE CONFUSION Very similar to the Panthercap (p. 38).
EDIBILITY Edible but must not be eaten raw.

Grey Spotted Amanita

▪ *Amanita excelsa* var. *spissa*
Cap 8–12cm, height 8–10cm

SYNONYM *Amanita spissa*.
DESCRIPTION The fleshy cap is convex at first,
later flattening slightly. It is grey-brown or grey
and covered in greyish patches or warts, the
remains of the universal veil. The cylindrical
stem is solid, greyish white, covered in brown
down or small scales below the floppy ring,
and ending in a bulb whose faintly perceptible
scales are the remains of the volva. The white
flesh is said to have a faint smell of kohlrabi.
HABITAT Under coniferous and deciduous
trees. Summer to autumn.
POSSIBLE CONFUSION Similar to *A. excelsa*
var. *excelsa*, which has the same common name
but is taller, has a smaller bulb at the base of
the stem and has a smaller ring. May also be
confused with the Panthercap (p. 38).
EDIBILITY Not edible.

Deathcap ▪ *Amanita phalloides*

Cap 5–15cm, height 8–12cm

DESCRIPTION The fleshy cap is convex at first,
later flattening. It is smooth in dry weather,
sticky when wet. The colour varies considerably
from olive to pale almond-green, yellowish
green and even white. The thick stem ends
in a ragged volva covering a large, smooth
bulb. The stem is solid at first, later becoming
hollow; like the crowded gills and spores, it is
white, though sometimes covered in greyish or
ochre tufts. The volva is always present, even
in mature specimens (a distinctive feature).
The membranous ring is striated. The white
flesh develops a strong, sickly-sweet smell.
HABITAT Under trees or in grass. Summer to
autumn.
EDIBILITY **Deadly poisonous**. The Deathcap
accounts for 95% of all fatal mushroom
poisonings.

Panther Cap ▪ *Amanita pantherina*
Cap 8–15cm, height 8–10cm

DESCRIPTION The large cap is convex at first, later flattening completely or even becoming slightly upturned. It is nut-brown to olive-brown in colour and covered in small, pure white warts that are uniformly distributed. The margin is striated at the edge. The tall, cylindrical white stem is ringed with ridges at the base, the topmost of which is like a collar (a distinctive feature). The volva and floppy ring high up the stem disappear in older specimens. The crowded gills and the spores are white. The flesh is white and thin.
HABITAT In deciduous woods. Autumn.
POSSIBLE CONFUSION Similar to The Blusher (p. 36) and Grey Spotted Amanita (p. 37).
EDIBILITY **Poisonous.**

False Deathcap ▪ *Amanita citrina*
Cap 8–15cm, height 5–12cm

DESCRIPTION The large cap is hemispherical at first, later flattening to a shallow dish. It is pale yellow or greenish yellow, often covered in large off-white or ochre membranous patches, the remnants of the universal veil. The tall, cylindrical stem is irregularly grooved and striated above the ring. It is swollen at the base into a large bulb; this is separated from the rest of the stem by a pronounced ridge. The floppy, striated ring is well developed and persistent. The flesh is white, smelling of celery or raw potato. There is an all-white variety, var. *alba*, the Alba False Deathcap.
HABITAT In deciduous and coniferous woodland. Late summer and autumn.
EDIBILITY Not edible.

Destroying Angel 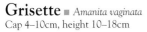 *Amanita virosa*
Cap 5–10cm, height 10–18cm

DESCRIPTION The large cap is strongly
hemispherical at first, later flattening slightly.
The whole fungus is pure white. The tall,
cylindrical stem may be straight or curved; it is
solid at first, then hollow. The white surface of
the stem is covered in bands of greyish-brown
fibrils arranged in a characteristic zigzag pattern.
The ring is fragile and disappears completely in
older specimens. The crowded gills are free and
the spores are white. The soft white flesh has a
sickly, unpleasant odour.

HABITAT Grows in association with Beech
Fagus sylvatica and with spruce trees at high
altitude. Autumn.

POSSIBLE CONFUSION The Fool's Mushroom
A. verna, also poisonous, looks very similar but
is found only in spring.

EDIBILITY **Deadly poisonous**.

Grisette ■ *Amanita vaginata*
Cap 4–10cm, height 10–18cm

SYNONYM *Amanitopsis vaginata*.

DESCRIPTION The fairly small cap can be
various shades of grey or grey-brown, but always
has a deeply furrowed margin. This, along
with the persistent volva sheathing the foot
and the absence of a ring, are the features that
distinguish the grisettes. The long, narrow stem
is white and may be covered in small scales. The
crowded gills and the spores are white. The flesh
is white and thin. Grisette and Tawny Grisette
(p. 40) were once classified in a separate genus
from the amanitas owing to the absence of a
ring. There is an all-white variety, var. *alba*.

HABITAT In woods and parks. Summer to
autumn.

EDIBILITY Edible but must not be eaten raw.

Tawny Grisette ■ *Amanita fulva*
Cap 4–10cm, height 10–18cm

SYNONYM *Amanitopsis fulva*.
DESCRIPTION The Tawny Grisette
may merely be a variety of the Grisette
(p. 39). Its main distinguishing feature is
the colour of the cap, which is brown to
golden brown. The cap is campanulate at
first, later flattening completely, usually
with a small central umbo. The margin is
deeply furrowed. The volva persists around
the foot. The long, narrow stem is hollow
and white, sometimes tinged with brown
in older specimens. The crowded gills and
the spores are white. The flesh is white
and thin.
HABITAT On acid soil, in damp places
under deciduous and coniferous trees.
Late spring to autumn.
EDIBILITY Edible but not to be eaten
raw.

Golden Waxcap
■ *Hygrocybe chlorophana*
Cap 3–6cm, height 4–7cm

DESCRIPTION The waxcaps are a group
of generally small gill fungi, in which
the cap, flesh and stem have a waxy or
slimy consistency, and the gills are widely
spaced and uneven; the cap and gills are
also slightly translucent. The Golden
Waxcap, as its name implies, has a pale
to bright yellow cap, gills and stem.
The cap is slimy, especially when wet,
convex at first, then flattening, with an
uneven margin and, sometimes, a
depressed centre. The flesh is whitish
to pale yellow, thin and very fragile. The
tall, sturdy stem is the same shade as the
cap or slightly paler. The spores are white.
HABITAT On grassland and in gardens. Jul–Oct.
EDIBILITY Not edible.

Heath Waxcap ■ *Hygrocybe laeta*
Cap 1.5–3.5cm, height 4–7cm

SYNONYM *Hygrophorus laetus*.
DESCRIPTION The orange-brown cap is
domed at first, slightly flattening in mature
specimens. It is deeply striated from the
margin along two-thirds of its surface; the
margin becomes ragged with age. The narrow
stem is the same colour as the cap or slightly
paler, with no ring. The decurrent gills are
greyish white, widely spaced and uneven. The
spores are white. The cap, stem and gill edges
are viscid.
HABITAT Often grows in large clusters,
on heaths, in the short grass of meadows, in
gardens where no artificial fertiliser has been
used, and among moss in moorland. Aug–Nov.
POSSIBLE CONFUSION Some forms of the
Parrot Waxcap (p. 44) are similar.
EDIBILITY Not edible.

Crimson Waxcap
■ *Hygrocybe punicea*
Cap 5–10cm, height 7–10cm

SYNONYM *Hygrophorus puniceus*.
DESCRIPTION This striking red
mushroom is one of the larger
waxcaps. The cap is a typical bell
shape, flattening and spreading
with age, and becoming irregular
but always retaining a central
umbo. The smooth, slightly
sticky, bright scarlet cuticle
yellows with age. The stem is
1–1.5cm thick and covered in
fibrils; it is the same colour as the
cap but white at the base. The

gills are adnexed and yellow, tinged with red. The flesh is whitish. The spores are white.
HABITAT Meadows and gardens. Autumn.
POSSIBLE CONFUSION The very similar Scarlet Waxcap (p. 42) is smaller and its stem is
yellow at the base.
EDIBILITY Not edible.

Scarlet Waxcap

■ *Hygrocybe coccinea*
Cap 2.5–5cm, height 2.5–7cm

SYNONYM *Hygrophorus coccineus*.
DESCRIPTION The cap is bell-shaped at first, flattening with age and even depressed in the centre, but always retaining a central umbo. The smooth, slightly sticky, usually bright scarlet cuticle, may be yellow or orange. The hollow stem is 1–1.5cm thick, often grooved down the centre; it is the same colour as the cap but yellow at the base. The waxy orange-red gills always have a yellow margin. The flesh is yellow to orange and the spores are white. HABITAT Meadows and gardens.

POSSIBLE CONFUSION Crimson Waxcap (p. 41) is very similar, but it is larger and its stem is white at the base. The Vermilion Waxcap *H. mineata* is another red waxcap with orange gills and flesh, preferring sandy soils.
EDIBILITY Not edible.

Meadow Waxcap

■ *Hygrocybe pratensis*
Cap 3–8cm, height 4–7cm

SYNONYMS *Camarophyllus pratensis*, *Cuphophyllus pratensis*.
DESCRIPTION The apricot- to salmon-coloured cap is convex at first, then flattening, with an uneven margin and, sometimes, a depressed centre, while retaining a wide umbo. The pale orange flesh is thick under the cap, thinner at the margin. The stem is fairly thick, thinning towards the base and often curved, smooth and friable; it is similar in colour to the cap but paler. The cream-coloured gills are widely spaced, irregular and deeply decurrent. The smell and taste are pleasant and mild. The spores are white. HABITAT Well-drained grassland and along paths; usually found at altitudes above 500m. Jul–Oct.
EDIBILITY Edible.

Blackening Waxcap

■ *Hygrocybe conica*
Cap 3–5cm, height 4–7cm

SYNONYMS Conical Waxcap,
H. nigrescens.
DESCRIPTION The cap remains conical
or bell-shaped, with a pointed umbo,
throughout its life. It is orange-red and
blackens in large patches, starting with
the umbo, as it ages. It is fragile and
often frayed at the edges. The stem is the
same colour as the cap when very young,
soon turning lemon-yellow, streaked with
red; it also blackens with age, starting at
the base. The flesh is whitish, blackening
with age, and thin and fragile. The spores
are white. The thick, widely spaced
gills are white, yellowing and becoming
covered in black patches when old.
HABITAT On grassland, in forest
clearings and in gardens. Jul–Oct.
EDIBILITY Not edible. Possibly
poisonous.

Pink Waxcap

■ *Hygrocybe calyptriformis*
Cap 3–8cm, height 4–7cm

SYNONYM Hooded Waxcap.
DESCRIPTION The cap of this beautiful
pink waxcap remains conical throughout
its life and is taller than it is wide, like
a hood. It pales in colour to lilac with
age. The margin is deeply fissured, frayed
and ragged, even when young. The stem
is smooth and white. The flesh is pink
under the cuticle, white elsewhere, thin
and fragile. The gills are widely spaced
and pale pink.
HABITAT On grassland, preferring
chalk or limestone soil on high ground.
Jul–Oct.
EDIBILITY Not edible.

Snowy Waxcap

■ *Hygrocybe virginea*
Cap 1–4cm, height 4–7cm

SYNONYMS *Cuphophyllus virgineus*, *Hygrophorus niveus*.
DESCRIPTION Despite its name, the Snowy Waxcap is not always pure white – the cap and stem may be pale ochre, or even have ochre or reddish patches. The cap is convex at first, then flattening and often becoming funnel-shaped when old. The flesh is white, and the gills are white or off-white, widely spaced and deeply decurrent. The tall, sturdy stem is the same colour as the cap or slightly paler. The spores are white.
HABITAT Found in large numbers on mossy lawns, and in grassy clearings in damp woods. Autumn to early winter.
POSSIBLE CONFUSION Easily confused with white funnel caps, especially the Ivory Funnel (p. 53), but that species has a thicker stem and the margin tends to be translucent.
EDIBILITY Edible.

Parrot Waxcap ■ *Hygrocybe psittacina*

Cap 2–4cm, height 5–8cm

DESCRIPTION The cap is often hemispherical and flat in the centre, but can also be a typical bell shape with a central umbo. It is slimy, translucent and glistening, especially in wet weather. The colour is bright yellow with contrasting patches of green, blue or orange, especially in the centre. The gills are widely spaced, yellow-green or orange, and do not reach as far as the striated margin. The cap and gills are slightly translucent. The flesh is thin and greenish yellow. The tall, sturdy stem is solid, later becoming hollow; it is the same colour as the cap at the top, paler towards the foot, and very slimy. The spores are white.
HABITAT In grassland at all altitudes. Summer to autumn.
EDIBILITY Not edible.

Ivory Woodwax

■ *Hygrophorus eburneus*
Cap 4–10cm, height 7–12cm

DESCRIPTION The slimy cap is white to ivory, with a slightly yellowish to pale brown central umbo, often flattening when older. The margin remains inrolled for a long time and becomes wavy as it flattens. The gills are white but may have orange to yellow patches. They are thick and widely spaced. The flesh is white, thin and fragile. The tall, sturdy stem is very often curved or sinuous, narrowing at the base, and granulose or floccose at the top; it is the same colour as the cap. The spores are white.

HABITAT Grows in large groups under deciduous trees, mainly Beech *Fagus sylvatica*, on non-acidic soils. Early to late autumn.

POSSIBLE CONFUSION Easily confused with other white species, including the Ivory Funnel (p. 53) and Snowy Waxcap (p. 44).

EDIBILITY Not edible.

Herald of Winter

■ *Hygrophorus hypothejus*
Cap 3–7cm, height 6–9cm

DESCRIPTION The coffee-brown to dirty-grey or olive, slimy cap is umbonate at first, flattening and slightly funnel-shaped when older. The margin remains inrolled for a long time, becoming wavy as it flattens; it is fibrillose and very slimy. The white gills gradually turn bright yellow-orange with age (a distinctive feature), and are thick, uneven and widely spaced. The flesh is white, yellow under the cuticle, and thick. The sturdy stem is straight and very sticky except at the top. It is white, turning orange-yellow.

HABITAT Grows in coniferous forests, mainly under pines, on acid soils. As its name implies, the Herald of Winter does not emerge until after the first frosts.

EDIBILITY Not edible.

Honey Fungus
■ *Armillaria mellea*
Cap 3–10cm, height 9–20cm

DESCRIPTION Grows in large clusters from a single tuft at the base. The convex, light brown or honey-coloured cap is covered in scales and fibrils of a darker shade. The flesh is firm and white. The stem is long and cylindrical, with a membranous white ring close to the top. Above the ring, it is covered in brown striations, whereas below it is smooth or speckled. The gills are whitish and decurrent, turning yellow and staining red with age.
HABITAT On coniferous and deciduous trees. It is parasitic on living trees, forming rhizomorphs that attack the tree under the bark, but it can also live on dead wood. Autumn.
EDIBILITY Edible, though not prized.

Sulphur Knight
■ *Tricholoma sulphureum*
Cap 3–10cm, height 4–7cm

SYNONYM Gas Agaric.
DESCRIPTION The whole fungus is sulphur-yellow. The cap is conical or hemispherical at first, then concave, depressed or with a small umbo in the centre. It is bright yellow, sometimes splashed with red patches. The yellow or brownish stem is covered in red fibrils, and is thicker and white at the base. The gills are thick, widely spaced and uneven. The thin flesh is yellow. The whole fungus has a sulphurous or gaseous smell.
HABITAT On acid soils in deciduous woods, especially under Beech *Fagus sylvatica*. Autumn.
POSSIBLE CONFUSION The edible Yellow Knight *T. equestre* is also yellow, but its cap is larger and the stem is short and thick.
EDIBILITY Not edible. Possibly poisonous.

Yellowing Knight

■ *Tricholoma sculpturatum*
Cap 3–6cm, height 4–7cm

SYNONYM *T. argyraceum*.
DESCRIPTION The cap is shallowly
convex, later flattening, and is
covered in grey-beige scales against
a cream-coloured background. The
margin yellows in older specimens.
The long, sturdy stem is smooth and
white, sometimes slightly greyish.
There is no ring. The off-white gills
are crowded and toothed, becoming
covered with yellow patches as they
age. The flesh smells strongly of meal
when cut or bruised; it is also white
but turns yellowish with age. The spores are white.
HABITAT Often found growing in large numbers on limestone soil in lowland
deciduous woods, or under conifers in mountainous regions. Summer and autumn.
EDIBILITY Edible, though not highly prized.

Tricholoma sciodes

Cap 5–10cm, height 2.5–7cm

DESCRIPTION This is one of a
number of *Tricholoma* species with
scaly grey caps. Though some are
edible, they are easily confused with
poisonous varieties. The cap is dry,
covered in greyish scales. The gills
are crowded, greyish pink and edged
with black (a distinctive feature).
The thick flesh is whitish and the
gills are white, as are the spores. The
stem is sturdy and white.
HABITAT Deciduous woods. Summer
and autumn.
POSSIBLE CONFUSION The Mousy
Tricholoma *T. myomyces*, the Girdled
Tricholoma *T. cingulatum* and the
Ashen Tricholoma *T. virgatum* are all similar species with scaly or fibrillose grey caps.
The Ashen Tricholoma is not edible and is suspect.
EDIBILITY Edible.

Birch Knight

■ *Tricholoma fulvum*
Cap 5–10cm, height 6–11cm

DESCRIPTION The fawn-coloured cap of this large mushroom spreads from a shallow, convex shape when young to depressed in the centre with a wavy margin when old; it is smooth but may have a central umbo. The crowded gills are pale yellow, showing patches of dirty red as they age. The sturdy stem is straight or curved and may be spindle-shaped (narrowing at the top and bottom). It is the same colour as the cap or sometimes yellower. The flesh is white in the cap and characteristically yellow in the stem. The flavour is bitter. The spores are white.

HABITAT Frequently, but not always, under birches, on damp acidic soil. Jun–Oct.
EDIBILITY Not edible.

Tricholoma ustaloides

Cap 6–10cm, height 4–7cm

DESCRIPTION The smooth reddish-brown to ochre cap is glistening and slimy when wet. It has a shallow dome shape when young, becoming flatter with a wavy margin when old. It is smooth and may have a central umbo. The crowded gills are white, showing patches of rust colour as they age. The sturdy stem is white at the top under the cap and dark brown further down. There is no ring. The flesh is white and bitter, smelling strongly of flour or cucumber. The spores are white.

HABITAT Under deciduous trees. Autumn.

POSSIBLE CONFUSION Burnt Knight *T. ustale* is similar but has a darker cap.

EDIBILITY Not considered edible, although it is eaten in parts of Mexico.

St George's Mushroom

■ *Calocybe gambosa*
Cap 5–15cm, height 5–20cm

DESCRIPTION The dove-grey to off-white domed cap, occasionally with yellowish or greyish patches, is often pitted or scarred. The white flesh is thick and firm, especially under the centre of the cap, and smells strongly of meal. The crowded off-white gills are small and thin in relation to the cap. The white stem is thick and fleshy, fibrillose at the top and striped below, and lacks a ring. The spores are white.
HABITAT On grassland, especially in areas enriched with mushroom compost. One of the few edible spring mushrooms, appearing around St George's Day (23 Apr), hence its common name.
EDIBILITY Edible and delicious. Sold in French markets. It is said to have hypoglycaemic properties, making it good for diabetics.

Violet Domecap

■ *Calocybe ionides*
Cap 2–4cm, height 4–6cm

SYNONYMS Lilac Fairhead Mushroom, *Rugosomyces ionides*.
DESCRIPTION This is another member of the tricholoma family, but along with the St George's Mushroom (*above*) is classified in a separate genus. Its lilac cap and stem are distinctive. The cap is hemispherical but flattens out in older specimens. It is smooth and fibrillose, almost velvety and slightly frayed at the margin. The crowded gills are cream-coloured or pale yellow. The stem, which later becomes hollow, is tall in relation to the cap and white under the gills. The spores are white.
HABITAT Grows in isolation in mixed woods. Summer and autumn.
POSSIBLE CONFUSION May be mistaken for other purple-capped species such as the Lilac Bonnet (p. 66).
EDIBILITY Not edible.

Plums and Custard

■ *Tricholomopsis rutilans*
Cap 5–12cm, height 7–12cm

DESCRIPTION The cap is hemispherical, flattening when older. It has a velvety texture and is densely covered with plum-coloured fibrils against a yellow background. The gills are also egg-yellow and fairly crowded. The flesh, which often has a bitter taste, is pale to bright yellow. The sturdy stem, which thickens at the base, is also pale yellow and covered in red fibrils, though these are less dense than on the cap. The spores are white.

HABITAT Grows in clumps on rotten pine logs and at the base of pine trunks. Late summer to autumn.

EDIBILITY The common name that aptly describes the colouring of this species is slightly misleading, as the fungus is not edible. Suspect.

Whitelaced Shank

■ *Megacollybia platyphylla*
Cap 8–20cm, height 3–8cm

SYNONYMS *Collybia platyphylla, Oudemansiella platyphylla, Tricholomopsis platyphylla.*

DESCRIPTION The dove-grey cap has the distinctive feature of tearing deeply into shreds in mature specimens, especially in dry weather. It is hemispherical, flattening and becoming depressed in the centre. The gills are off-white, and are so large that when the mushroom is bisected they are seen to occupy almost all of the space of the cap, leaving room for only a thin strip of flesh. The tall stem is off-white, fibrillose and shows faint signs of the fugacious ring. The fungus produces long white rhizomorphs.

HABITAT Broadleaf woodland, on rotting leaves and wood, mainly oak. Has a long fruiting season, from spring to late autumn

EDIBILITY Not edible.

Trooping Funnel

■ *Clitocybe geotropa*
Cap 6–20cm, height 10–20cm

SYNONYM Monk's Head.
DESCRIPTION The funnel caps are
distinguished by a deeply depressed cap
and decurrent gills when mature. This large
species retains a small central umbo. The
whole fungus is pale brown to flesh-coloured,
and the wide, dry cap resembles the hood
of a Franciscan friar, hence its alternative
common name. The cream or beige gills are
strongly decurrent. The flesh is white, thick
under the cuticle and thinning at the margin;
it smells of bitter almonds. The fibrous stem
is the same colour as the cap and ringless,
often ending in a club shape at the base.
HABITAT Grows in rings or rows in well-lit
broadleaf forests, clearings and beside paths.
Autumn.
EDIBILITY Edible.

Clouded Funnel

■ *Clitocybe nebularis*
Cap 8–20cm, height 8–14cm

DESCRIPTION The dark grey cap is convex
when young, flattening, turning paler and
becoming only slightly depressed when
mature. The margin stays inrolled for a
long time. The beige to pale yellow gills are
crowded and decurrent. The flesh is soft and
white. The greyish-white stem is covered in
darker grey fibrils; it is bulbous at the foot,
which is normally deeply embedded in leaf
litter. The spores are white.
HABITAT Grows in rings in deciduous and
coniferous forests. Late autumn and winter.
POSSIBLE CONFUSION Resembles the
poisonous Livid Pinkgill (p. 71), but lacks
that species' pinkish tinge to the gills.
EDIBILITY Edible but too easily confused
with poisonous species.

Common Funnel

■ *Clitocybe gibba*
Cap 4–10cm, height 4–6cm

SYNONYMS C. *infundibuliformis*, *Infundibulicybe gibba*.

DESCRIPTION The cap is deeply inrolled at first, then deeply funnel-shaped, often with a very slight central umbo. The margin is wavy in older specimens. The colour of the cap varies considerably from cream or beige at the margin to pale brown in the centre, or the whole cap may be uniformly pale brown or reddish brown. The white gills are crowded and very decurrent. The flesh is thin and white. The narrow stem is straight, and is off-white or pale reddish brown; its base is surrounded by a mesh of white mycelium. The smell is pleasant.

HABITAT Coniferous and deciduous forests, often forming large clumps. Summer and autumn.

EDIBILITY Edible.

Aniseed Funnel

■ *Clitocybe odora*
Cap 4–8cm, height 4–6cm

DESCRIPTION The matte cap of this small funnel cap is slightly depressed in mature specimens but remains convex throughout its life, initially with an inrolled margin. The colour is a distinctive blue-green, turning greyish green or greyish brown in older specimens. The gills are slightly decurrent and off-white, turning greyish green when older. The flesh is soft and white, tasting and smelling strongly of aniseed, another distinctive feature. The stem is long, fibrillose and whitish, or sometimes the same colour as the cap, with a felty covering of mycelium at the base.

HABITAT Mainly associated with Beech *Fagus sylvatica*, birch and spruce trees. Summer and autumn.

EDIBILITY Edible but has a strong aniseed flavour.

Ivory Funnel

■ *Clitocybe rivulosa*
Cap 2–4cm, height 6–9cm

SYNONYM *C. dealbata.*
DESCRIPTION This is one of several all-white funnel caps (some of which are edible, some poisonous), making it hard for the amateur to identify with certainty. The cap flattens in older specimens, never becoming truly funnel-shaped and retaining a central umbo. It often appears to be covered in frost, and the margin is sometimes translucent. The texture is matt and silky. The crowded white gills are slightly decurrent. The flesh is thin and white, and smells strongly of flour. The thick stem is sometimes slightly curved and elastic; it is white, off-white or beige, and white at the top.
HABITAT Grows in clumps or rings in pastures, on lawns and in hedgerows. Summer and autumn.
POSSIBLE CONFUSION Other white funnel caps and Snowy Waxcap (p. 44).
EDIBILITY **Deadly poisonous**.

The Goblet

■ *Pseudoclitocybe cyathiformis*
Cap 3–7cm, height 6–10cm

SYNONYM *Cantharellula cyathiformis.*
DESCRIPTION The small, round cap is hygrophanous, varying in colour depending on the degree of humidity in the atmosphere from dark grey-brown when wet to paler brown when dry. The cap remains inrolled even when mature. The gills are white and forked, with ragged edges. The flesh is thin and spongy. The long, sturdy stem is grey or whitish, striated with paler fibrils; it is often sinuate or curved, and is covered in fluffy white mycelium at the base.
HABITAT On coniferous and deciduous deadwood, such as mossy logs. Autumn.
EDIBILITY Not edible.

Club Foot

■ *Ampulloclitocybe clavipes*
Cap 4–7cm, height 6–8cm

SYNONYM *Clitocybe clavipes*.
DESCRIPTION The grey to dark brown cap is paler towards the margin; it flattens and then becomes slightly depressed in the centre. It is smooth, slightly greasy in texture when moist, and has an inrolled margin. The gills are deeply decurrent, fairly crowded, and whitish, cream or yellow. The stem is narrow at the top, thickening at the base into a club shape that can vary from barely noticeable to extremely pronounced. It is pale grey to cream, and is covered in fibrils. The flesh is thin and white, and has a pleasant smell.
HABITAT Grows singly or in groups on acid soil under deciduous and coniferous trees. Summer and autumn.
EDIBILITY **Poisonous**, especially if consumed with alcohol.

Velvet Shank ■ *Flammulina velutipes* Cap 2–8cm, height 1–10cm

SYNONYM *Collybia velutipes*.
DESCRIPTION The cap is flat and slimy, convex or slightly depressed, and pale orange-brown with a paler margin. The stem is thin and woody, yellowish at the top and much darker towards the base, and is entirely covered in a velvety down. It has no ring. The flesh is yellowish white and thin, and the spores are white.
HABITAT Grows in clumps, clusters and large numbers on rotting wood, especially that of willows, Beech *Fagus sylvatica* and Apple *Malus domestica*. Late autumn to midwinter in temperate regions.
POSSIBLE CONFUSION The poisonous *Galerina autumnalis* also grows in clusters on wood, but it has a thin ring and brown spores.
EDIBILITY Edible. Cultivated in China, Korea and Japan, where it is known as Enokitake.

The Deceiver ■ *Laccaria laccata*
Cap 2–6cm, height 6–10cm

DESCRIPTION The Deceiver gets its name from its wide variety of forms and coloration. The cap is convex, sometimes flattened, often with a central depression and with a smooth, striated or grooved margin. The cap changes colour from dark brown to pale reddish brown, especially as it dries out. The adnate or decurrent gills are thick, almost flesh-coloured or the same colour as the cap, and generally widely spaced. The stem is thin and sometimes tapers at the base. It is tough and fibrous, and is the same colour as the cap. The flesh is thin and the same colour as the cap. The spores are white.
HABITAT Mixed woods. Forms mycorrhiza. Summer to autumn.
POSSIBLE CONFUSION Wood Woollyfoot (p. 57), but that species has a hairy stem.
EDIBILITY Edible.

Amethyst Deceiver

■ *Laccaria amethystina* Cap 3–7cm, height 6–9cm

DESCRIPTION This striking purple fungus was once considered a variety of The Deceiver (*above*). The cap is convex, sometimes flattened and often with a central depression, and has a smooth, striated, irregular margin. It becomes paler as it dries out. The adnate gills are thick and are the same colour as the cap. They are generally widely spaced. The thin, fibrous stem is the same colour as the cap. The flesh is thin and the same colour as the cap. The spores are white.
HABITAT Grows in mixed woods, mainly on high ground. Summer to autumn.
POSSIBLE CONFUSION May be mistaken for other purple species, such as the poisonous Lilac Bonnet (p. 66) or Lilac Fibrecap, a violet variety of the White Fibrecap (p. 83).
EDIBILITY Edible.

Russet Toughshank

■ *Collybia dryophila*
Cap 1–7.5cm, height 6–9cm

SYNONYM *Gymnopus dryophilus*.
DESCRIPTION The tawny or reddish-brown cap has a incurving margin when young, this becoming irregular and wavy as it matures. The cuticle is slightly greasy. The crowded whitish, pinkish or yellowish gills are adnexed or free. The thick flesh is white, and yellow under the cuticle. The sturdy stem is fibrous or smooth, whitish just under the cap and darkening below. It is solid at first but later hollow. The parasitic fungus *Syzygospora mycetophila* sometimes attacks Russet Toughshank, producing pale growths on the stem, gills and cap.
HABITAT On twigs and leaf litter. Spring to late autumn.
EDIBILITY Edible, but the stem is tough and should be discarded.

Spindle Toughshank

■ *Collybia fusipes* Cap 3–12cm, height 8–15cm

SYNONYM Spindleshank, *Gymnopus fusipes*.
DESCRIPTION The fungi of the toughshank family all have long, root-like stems. The light brown cap of the Spindle Toughshank is hemispherical at first, later flattening, with an irregular margin that is inrolled in young specimens. The flesh is thick and pale brown. The most distinctive feature of the fungus is the long stem, which is striated and sometimes splits, and may vary in colour from off-white to brown. It is swollen in the middle, and ends in a long, tapering, dark brown, spindly foot. The gills are whitish, darkening to rusty brown. The spores are white.
HABITAT Grows in large clusters on tree stumps (especially oak) in broadleaf woods. Summer to autumn.
EDIBILITY Edible when young.

Wood Woollyfoot

■ *Collybia peronata* Cap 3–6cm, height 7–9cm

SYNONYMS *Gymnopus peronata, Marasmius peronatus*.

DESCRIPTION The coffee-brown to ochre, yellowish or beige cap is umbonate at first, flattening when older. It is smooth or slightly wrinkled, with a wavy margin. The widely spaced, irregular off-white gills are adnexed and gradually turn brownish. The flesh is yellowish and tastes peppery. The tall, straight stem is thickly covered in spiky white or pale yellow hairs towards the base (a distinctive feature), hence the species' common name. The spore print is white, cream or yellowish.

HABITAT In coniferous and deciduous woods. Summer and autumn.

POSSIBLE CONFUSION The Deceiver (p. 55) looks similar but the stem is not covered in hairs.

EDIBILITY Not edible owing to its peppery flesh.

Spotted Toughshank

■ *Collybia maculata*
Cap 6–15cm, height 7–13cm

SYNONYM *Rhodocollybia maculata*.

DESCRIPTION The cap is hemispherical at first, flattening when older. It is whitish and splashed with rust-coloured patches, hence the species' name. The margin is usually inrolled in young specimens. The very crowded gills are sinuate, toothed and white, though usually also splashed with rust-coloured patches. The flesh is white and tastes bitter. The tall, straight, fibrous stem is fairly thick,

white at the top but with one or more dark brown patches that look like stains in the lower part (a distinctive feature). There is no ring. The spore print is white, cream or yellowish.

HABITAT Grows in isolation or in small groups under conifers. Summer and autumn.

EDIBILITY Not edible.

Butter Cap ■ *Collybia butyracea*
Cap 3–7cm, height 6–9cm

SYNONYM *Rhodocollybia butyracea*.
DESCRIPTION The yellowish-brown cap
is umbonate at first, always remaining
hemispherical but darkening at the margin.
It has a greasy or buttery texture, especially in
the centre, hence the species' common name.
It is hygrophanous, turning paler in dry weather.
The white or cream-coloured gills are crowded.
The flesh is watery and grey-brown. The stem is
straight and reddish brown, often with the fluffy
white mycelium visible at the base.
HABITAT In pinewoods and under some
broadleaf trees, among dead leaves and needles.
It prefers rich, neutral soil. Var. *asema*, a variety
with a darker cap that is paler at the margin,
grows only under Beech *Fagus sylvatica*. Autumn.
EDIBILITY Not edible.

Delicatula integrella
Cap 1–1.5cm, height 2–3cm

SYNONYM *Omphalia integrella*.
DESCRIPTION This tiny, fragile
species is one of a group of delicate
fungi with small, bell-shaped
caps and long, thin white stems.
Delicatula integrella is entirely snowy
white. The cap is bell-shaped at
first, flattening out but always with
a central umbo, and eventually
becoming slightly upturned at
the edges. The white gills are
forked, folded and widely spaced.
The tall white stem is translucent
and ringless. The base is slightly
bulbous.
HABITAT In tufts or groups on
rotting wood or plant matter. Summer to autumn.
POSSIBLE CONFUSION The Twig Parachute (p. 60) looks similar but the lower half of the
stem is pale brown.
EDIBILITY Not edible.

Fairy Ring Champignon

■ *Marasmius oreades*
Cap 2–5cm, height 4–6cm

DESCRIPTION This little mushroom is quite distinctive owing to its conical, umbonate cap and irregular, widely spaced gills. The cap is hygrophanous, being entirely brown in wet weather and beige in dry weather, but always with a darker central umbo. The flesh is thin and the same colour as the gills, which are beige, turning reddish ochre.
HABITAT On all types of grassland, from meadows to parks and gardens, growing in rings from a radiating mycelium. Spring to autumn.
EDIBILITY Edible and delicious except for the tough stem. When raw, it apparently contains hydrocyanic acid, which has restorative qualities in minute quantities. Easy to dry and preserve.

Pearly Parachute

■ *Marasmius wynnei*
Cap 2–6cm, height 3–8cm

SYNONYMS Mrs Wynne's Mushroom, M. *globularis*.
DESCRIPTION This small all-white mushroom is slightly translucent. As in all members of the genus *Marasmius*, the cap, which has a pale brown umbo and is slightly striated, remains hemispherical or slightly conical throughout its life. The white gills sometimes have a greyish or lilac tint. The flesh is thick and white, but yellow under the cuticle. The narrow stem is white and powdery at the top, turning grey or orange-brown near the base. The white flesh smells of bitter almonds. The spores are white.
HABITAT Grows individually or in small groups on leaf or pine-needle litter and on grass verges. Autumn.
EDIBILITY Not edible.

Collared Parachute

■ *Marasmius rotula* Cap 2–6cm, height 2–4cm

DESCRIPTION The white cap of this tiny, delicate fungus is divided into grooved sections like a parachute, and its centre is grey and umbilicate. The white gills are widely spaced, separated from stem by a collar. The flesh is almost non-existent. The very thin, wiry stem is grey at the top and turns black further down. The spores are white.
HABITAT Grows in small clusters on the damp twigs of deciduous trees. Summer and autumn.
POSSIBLE CONFUSION The parachute fungi contains several small species with pale caps and dark, wiry stems, including the Horsehair Parachute M. *androsaceus*, whose cap is dark to pale brown, never completely white, and whose glistening, wiry stem is entirely black.
EDIBILITY Not edible.

Twig Parachute

■ *Marasmiellus ramealis*
Cap 1–2cm, height 0.4–1.5cm

DESCRIPTION The translucent cream-coloured or beige cap is campanulate when the fungus is immature, flattening out as it matures, with an even margin. The widely spaced gills are white, cream or pinkish brown, ragged, irregular and free. The narrow stem is slightly eccentric and incurving in taller specimens, to ensure the cap remains parallel to the ground for optimum spore distribution; it is covered in small scales or flakes and is whitish at the top, darkening to sepia below the midpoint. There is no ring. The spores are white.
HABITAT Grows in groups along the length of damp dead twigs or branches of deciduous trees. Autumn.
POSSIBLE CONFUSION *Delicatula integrella* (p. 58).
EDIBILITY Not edible.

Rooting Shank ■ *Xerula radicata*
Cap 2–10cm, height 20–30cm

SYNONYMS *Collybia radicata*, *Mucidula radicata*, *Oudemansiella radicata*.

DESCRIPTION The cap is coffee-coloured or grey-brown, viscous, and often folded over on itself or irregular in shape. The gills are wide and white. The stem is exceptionally long and deeply embedded in the ground in a long, pointed, root-like tip, hence the species' common name; the section above ground is greyish white. The spores are white. There are several varieties, including the all-white var. *alba*, one with a dark edge to the gills (var. *marginata*) and one with pink gills (var. *roseophylla*).

HABITAT On rotting wood, often pieces that are buried underground. Autumn.

EDIBILITY Edible but of no culinary interest.

Tawny Funnel
■ *Lepista flaccida*
Cap 4–10cm, height 5–10cm

DESCRIPTION The cap of this mushroom is slightly convex at first, eventually becoming deeply funnel-shaped. It is reddish brown, russet or ochraceous, very often with an eccentric stem and a very sinuous margin. The stem is very short and the same colour as the cap. The gills are paler than the cap but similar in colour and deeply decurrent. The flesh is thick under the cap and thin at the margin. The spores are white.

HABITAT On leaf litter under deciduous trees. Autumn.

POSSIBLE CONFUSION The Inside Out Agaric (*L. inversa*, *Clitocybe inversa*) is similar but grows under conifers; considered by some authorities to be a variety of the same species.

EDIBILITY Edible, although there are differing opinions as to its quality and the stem is too tough to eat.

Wood Blewit
■ *Lepista nuda*
Cap 5–15cm, height 6–12cm

SYNONYMS Blue Foot, Blue Stalk, *Tricholoma nudum*.
DESCRIPTION The fleshy, convex cap is dry, and pale brown in the centre with a violet tint. The gills are crowded, sinuate and bright violet, fading as the fungus ages. The flesh is thick and pale lilac, fading to white in older specimens. Both the cuticle and flesh of the sturdy stem always remain violet. The stem is covered with soft white or silvery fibrils. The spores are pale greyish lilac.
HABITAT Grows in coniferous and deciduous woods, often forming large rings. Autumn.
POSSIBLE CONFUSION The Lesser Blue-Foot (*L. sordida*) is half the size and grows in woods and cultivated grassland. It is also edible.
EDIBILITY Edible and delicious. Sold commercially.

Porcelain Fungus
■ *Oudemansiella mucida*
Cap 3–10cm, height 3–8cm

SYNONYM *Armillaria mucida*.
DESCRIPTION This beautiful, translucent, pure white fungus is highly distinctive. The white cap, which is always hemispherical, is occasionally tinted with greenish grey in the centre and is covered with a slimy coating that gives it a brilliant shine. The margin is often wrinkled or furrowed. The large, widely spaced gills are white. The stem is often curving, to ensure that the cap remains parallel to the ground so that the spores are shed correctly. The flesh is thin and white. There is always a distinct white ring. The spores are pale cream.
HABITAT Grows in large numbers on the branches, trunk and stumps of dead or decaying Beech *Fagus sylvatica*. Autumn.
EDIBILITY Not edible.

Conifercone Cap
■ *Baeospora myosura*
Cap 1–3cm, height 2–4cm

SYNONYM Mousetail Collybia, *Collybia conigena*.
DESCRIPTION The cap is hemispherical, flattening as it ages, sometimes with a small central umbo. The ochre to date-brown cuticle is smooth and dry, paler at the margin. The gills are white or pale grey and very crowded. The flesh is pale brown and thin. The sturdy stem has the width and consistency of a mouse's tail (hence the species' alternative common name), is paler than the cap and is covered in powdery white scales; it tapers to a root-like structure covered in stiff hairs that embeds itself in the substrate.
HABITAT As its name implies, the Conifercone Cap grows exclusively on pine or spruce cones, sometimes on individual scales. Autumn and early winter.
POSSIBLE CONFUSION Pinecone Cap (p. 69) is similar but usually found in spring.
EDIBILITY Not edible.

Grooved Bonnet
■ *Mycena polygramma*
Cap 1–5cm, height 5–20cm

DESCRIPTION Fungi of the genus *Mycena* have small, conical caps and long, narrow stems. The mouse-coloured cap of the Grooved Bonnet is conical at first, opening out like an umbrella. It is covered in powdery, shiny scales in dry weather or is slightly viscous in wet weather. The centre of the cap is darker than the rest. The gills are white, greyish or pinkish, sometimes splashed with brown patches. The tall stem is straight and narrow, rigid, hollow and brittle, with long, vertical silver-grey striations in mature specimens. There is a pure white variety (var. *alba*), and a smaller variety (var. *pumila*) that grows on living wood.
HABITAT On logs or buried wood. Spring.
EDIBILITY Not edible.

Common Bonnet
■ *Mycena galericulata*
Cap 1–8cm, height 6–9cm

DESCRIPTION The bell shape of the cap of this bonnet is grey-brown, paler in dry weather and viscous when wet, and with a darker colour on the central umbo. The margin remains paler and the whole surface is thinly striated. The flesh is white, with a very unpleasant rancid smell. The gills are white or faintly pink, interlinked by veins. The long, rigid stem is hollow and brittle; it is grey-brown, becoming darker brown at the base. It has a tapering, root-like extension at the base that can be as long as 10cm.

HABITAT Grows in large clumps on logs or rotten wood of broadleaf trees. Summer and autumn.
EDIBILITY Not edible.

Milking Bonnet
■ *Mycena galopus*
Cap 0.5–2cm, height 5–9cm

DESCRIPTION The cap may be smooth or furrowed, and is always campanulate with a central umbo; it is conical at first, flattening to hemispherical when older. Its colour varies considerably from ochraceous brown to grey (var. *nigra* illustrated), but it is always darker in the centre and the margin is striated. The flesh is thin and whitish. The long, rigid grey stem is hollow, brittle and translucent. The most distinctive feature of the species is that, when the stem is broken, it exudes a white milky liquid. The spores are white. There is a pure white variety (var. *candida*).
HABITAT On leaf litter in mixed woods and hedgerows. Summer and autumn.
EDIBILITY Not edible.

Burgundydrop Bonnet

■ *Mycena haematopus*
Cap 3–7cm, height 6–9cm

SYNONYMS Big Blood Stalk, Bleeding Mycena.
DESCRIPTION The colour of the cap and stem
are extremely variable in this fungus, ranging
from pale reddish brown to rose madder. The
cap margin is toothed and slightly striated.
The white to flesh-coloured gills are adnate
and crowded, with a small decurrent tooth. The
flesh is pale, turning blood-red; it is thick in
the centre of the cap and thin elsewhere. The
stem is similar in colour to the cap, later turning
paler; it exudes a blood-red juice when broken.
HABITAT Grows in tufts on the dead twigs and
stumps of deciduous trees in lowland areas, and
of coniferous trees on high ground. Autumn.
POSSIBLE CONFUSION Bleeding Bonnet
M. *sanguinolenta* has a paler cap and exudes
paler liquid.
EDIBILITY Not edible.

Saffrondrop Bonnet

■ *Mycena crocata*
Cap 0.5–2.5cm, height 6–11cm

DESCRIPTION The cap is umbonate at first,
later flattening into the shape of a coolie hat.
It is generally orange to grey-brown but may be
off-white, and is always darker in the centre.
The cap margin is paler and striated. The gills
are crowded and white, often splashed with
orange patches. The flesh is thick and white,
but yellow under the cuticle. The tall, brittle
stem is translucent and orange to beige, or
sometimes pure orange. The base is surrounded
by a white and orange mycelium. The stem
exudes an orange milk when broken. The spores
are white.
HABITAT Grows singly or in groups on dead
wood, especially Beech *Fagus sylvatica*, in
sheltered spots. Summer and autumn.
EDIBILITY Not edible.

Lilac Bonnet ■ *Mycena pura*
Cap 2–5cm, height 4–7cm

DESCRIPTION The cap is convex at first, then flattening, sometimes leaving a small central umbo. The margin is striated in old specimens. The cap is hygrophanous, so the colour varies considerably depending on the weather: it may be paler to deeper brown with violet hues, and is shiny and sticky when wet (var. *rosea* illustrated). The white gills are sometimes shaded with violet, and are thick, uneven and widely spaced. The flesh is thin and white. The tall, sturdy stem is straight, ringless and silky or fibrillose, thickening slightly towards the base.

HABITAT On leaf litter in mixed woods. Summer and autumn.
POSSIBLE CONFUSION May be mistaken for other purple or lilac species such as Amethyst Deceiver (p. 55) and Blackedge Bonnet (*below*).
EDIBILITY **Poisonous**.

Blackedge Bonnet
■ *Mycena pelianthina*
Cap 2–6cm, height 6–9cm

DESCRIPTION The cap remains convex, flattening to become hemispherical, sometimes with a small central umbo. It can be various shades of violet and grey, paler at the margin, which is striated in older specimens. The violet gills are thick, uneven and widely spaced, edged with a deeper stripe of purple. The whitish flesh is thick under the centre of the cap and smells strongly of radishes. The tall, sturdy stem is straight, firm and shiny, similar in colour to the cap but paler. The spores are white.

HABITAT In clumps, on or around stumps of coniferous trees. Autumn.
POSSIBLE CONFUSION Lilac Bonnet (*above*) is very similar but its gills do not have a deeper purple strip along their margin.
EDIBILITY **Poisonous**.

Clustered Bonnet

■ *Mycena inclinata* Cap 1–4cm, height 4–12cm

SYNONYM Stinking Mycena.
DESCRIPTION The creamy-grey or creamy-brown campanulate cap, which may exhibit red patches, never flattens and is viscous in wet weather. The colour darkens in the centre. The off-white flesh is thin and the white gills are crowded. The long, thin, brittle stem is sometimes bent or curved to ensure that the cap remains parallel to the ground for efficient spore release. It is white at the top, gradually darkening through yellow and orange to brown at the base. The most distinctive feature is the unpleasant smell, said to resemble rancid fat.
HABITAT Grows in large tufts on rotten logs and wood of deciduous trees, mainly oaks. Autumn.
EDIBILITY Not edible.

Yellowleg Bonnet

■ *Mycena epipterygia*
Cap 1–2cm, height 5–7cm

SYNONYM Fern Mycena.
DESCRIPTION The yellow or ochre cap is hemispherical or conical, striated with a darker shade or deeply grooved with a ragged margin. It is covered with a detachable, viscous, gelatinous film that ensures the cap is shiny in all weathers. Another distinctive feature is the hollow, cylindrical stem, which is tall, slender and bright yellow; it is covered with the same gelatinous film as the cap. The gills are whitish and the spore print is white. The taste and smell are floury and slightly rancid.
HABITAT Widely distributed, growing on mossy lawns, in mixed woods, among pine needles, and on the decaying wood of deciduous trees. Summer and autumn.
EDIBILITY Not edible.

Orange Mosscap

■ *Rickenella fibula* Cap 3–7cm, height 6–9cm

SYNONYMS Orange Nail Fungus, *Omphalina fibula*.

DESCRIPTION The bright orange cap is parachute-shaped with a deep central depression. The odourless whitish flesh is so thin as to be almost non-existent, and at the cap margin the gills can be seen through it. The curved, thick orange gills are widely spaced, decurrent, and cream-coloured or pale yellow. The tall, slender stem tapers at the base, is translucent and is the same colour as, or paler than, the cap. The nail-shaped silhouette of the fungus is the reason for its alternative common name.

HABITAT On damp mossy lawns, in bogs and in damp forests. Has a long growing season, from late spring to autumn.

EDIBILITY Not edible.

Powdery Piggyback

■ *Asterophora lycoperdoides*
Cap 1–2cm, height 1–2cm

SYNONYM Star-bearing Powdercap.

DESCRIPTION The small *Asterophora* genus contains only 2 species, both parasitic on milkcaps (*Lactarius*, pp. 24–27) and brittlegills (*Russula*, pp. 28–32). In the Powdery Piggyback, the cap is white at first, soon becoming thickly covered with a light brown powder; this is a layer of asexual spores, known as chlamydospores, which are its main form of reproduction. As a result, the white gills of the fungus are degenerate and deformed, so that the fungus appears to be have none and resembles a Common Puffball (p. 129). The flesh is dark brown to grey, and the white stem is short.

HABITAT On the rotting remains of the Blackening Brittlegill (p. 28) in damp weather conditions. Autumn.

EDIBILITY Not edible.

Pinecone Cap

■ *Strobilurus tenacellus*
Cap 1–3cm, height 2–6cm

DESCRIPTION The cap is hemispherical and slightly ragged at the edges, brownish yellow to tobacco-coloured and paler in the centre. The flesh is off-white and thin, with a bitter taste. The stem, which may be curved to allow the cap to remain parallel to the ground for efficient spore release, is slender, brittle and translucent white at the top, gradually darkening through yellow and brown to dark brown at the base.

HABITAT On pinecones. Mostly in the spring, occasionally later.

POSSIBLE CONFUSION Similar to the Conifercone Cap (p. 63), which has the same habitat but grows only in the autumn, and whose stem is not powdery.

EDIBILITY Not edible.

Bitter Oysterling

■ *Panellus stipticus*
Cap 1–3cm, height 1–4cm

SYNONYM Styptic Mushroom.

DESCRIPTION In the oysterlings, the caps are imbricated, meaning that they grow in a dense tuft superimposed on one another, and the stem is lateral (on one side) and very short. These are features of many of the fungi that grow on tree trunks or logs. In Bitter Oysterling the fan-shaped cap is ochraceous brown (although there is a variety of the species in which it is white). The gills are ochre or reddish, ending in a ring at the top of the short white stem. The flesh is tough and bitter. The spores are off-white.

HABITAT Grows in large numbers on deciduous trees, mainly oaks. Summer and autumn

EDIBILITY Not edible.

Olive Oysterling

▪ *Panellus serotinus*
Cap 1–3cm, height 1–4cm

SYNONYM Winter Panellus.
DESCRIPTION The smooth, shiny, fan-shaped cap is olive-green or yellowish green, or even off-white to brownish yellow, with a margin that remains inrolled or incurved its whole life. The crowded gills are pale off-white or buff and slightly decurrent. The short, thick stem is scaly and yellow, and is always darker than the gills. The flesh is tough and bitter, making the fungus inedible. The spores are off-white.
HABITAT On decayed wood of deciduous trees; has been found inside hollow logs in the snow. Late autumn to winter.
POSSIBLE CONFUSION The colour of the cap is so variable that the brown-capped variety is easily confused with the Elm Oyster Mushroom *Pleurotus ulmarius* (*Hypsizygus ulmarius*), but in that species the stem is white and much longer.
EDIBILITY Not edible.

Wrinkled Peach

▪ *Rhodotus palmatus*
Cap 2–8cm, height 2–5cm

DESCRIPTION The cap may resemble a wrinkled peach or apricot when looked at from above, although this does not mean it is good to eat. The cap is convex at first, then flattening, peach-coloured or saffron with apricot patches, wrinkled and occasionally heavily reticulated. The cuticle is covered with a layer of mucus that makes it glisten. The pink gills are often detached from the stem, forming a ring around it. The flesh is white or reddish orange and bitter. The stem is tall and slender, white then pinkish, often eccentric and sometimes lateral. The spore print is pink.
HABITAT In clumps on recently fallen deciduous deadwood, mainly Sweet Chestnut *Castanea sativa* and elm. Early autumn to winter.
EDIBILITY Not edible.

Livid Pinkgill

■ *Entoloma sinuatum*
Cap 3–7cm, height 6–9cm

SYNONYMS Lead Poisoner, Leaden
Pinkgill, *E. lividum, Rhodophyllus sinuatus.*
DESCRIPTION The hemispherical or
conical cap is leaden grey, eventually
becoming convex or flattened. The
margin remains inrolled for a long time.
It is sinuous, and becomes wavy in older
specimens. The flesh is white, thick in the
centre of the cap. The gills are uneven
and widely spaced, ranging from pale
yellow to pale pink in older specimens.
The spores are pink. The stem is fairly
thick, slightly swollen at the base, fibrillose and whitish, greying with age.
HABITAT In rings or small groups, sometimes in clumps with 1 or 2 specimens attached to
each other at the base, under deciduous trees. Late summer and autumn.
POSSIBLE CONFUSION Clouded Funnel (p. 51) but that species lacks a pink tinge to the
gills.
EDIBILITY **Poisonous**.

Shield Pinkgill

■ *Entoloma clypeatum*
Cap 3–10cm, height 6–13cm

DESCRIPTION The hemispherical cap is
grey, brownish grey or ochre, eventually
becoming convex with a central umbo.
It is hygrophanous, so turns darker in wet
weather. The margin remains inrolled and
is sinuous and irregular; it is often torn in
older specimens. The flesh is thick and
white, turning grey when wet, and smells
of meal. The gills are irregular and widely
spaced, whitish, then dirty pink. The
spores are pink. The tall stem is fibrillose
and whitish or grey, sometimes yellowing
at the base.
HABITAT Grows in rings or groups,
sometimes with 1 or 2 specimens attached to each other at the base, under Blackthorn
Prunus spinosa, hawthorn and plum trees. Spring.
EDIBILITY Edible, but easily confused with toxic species.

The Miller

■ *Clitopilus prunulus*
Cap 3–7cm, height 3–9cm

DESCRIPTION This all-white mushroom has a downy cap that flattens into an irregular shape. The margin remains inrolled for a long time, becoming curved and wavy as it flattens. The cap surface becomes irregular and may even be funnel-shaped. The strongly decurrent, widely spaced gills are off-white when young, turning pinkish as the spores mature. The flesh is thick but fragile, with a strong mealy odour, hence the species' common name. The sturdy white stem can vary in length from short to longish. The base is covered in fluffy cottony mycelium.

HABITAT In mixed woods, among heather and bilberry bushes. Summer to autumn.

EDIBILITY Edible, but too similar to poisonous white species to be safe for beginners.

Deer Shield

■ *Pluteus cervinus*
Cap 5–15cm, height 10–15cm

SYNONYMS Fawn Mushroom, *Pluteus atricapillus*.

DESCRIPTION The cap varies in colour from dark brown to fawn or light brown, and is covered in fibrils resembling the coat of a fallow deer or fawn. The margin remains inrolled for a long time. The flesh is thin and white, quite soft, and has a faint smell of radishes. The gills are white at first, turning pink when mature, and are free. The tall stem is striped with longitudinal fibrils that are white at first, later turning brown.

HABITAT Usually occurs singly, on heavily decayed wood. Spring to autumn.

EDIBILITY Edible but of no value.

Willow Shield ■ *Pluteus salicinus*
Cap 3–7cm, height 5–11cm

DESCRIPTION The grey-brown or greyish-green cap is convex to shield-shaped, being depressed around the darker central umbo; it is smooth or fibrillose. The crowded white gills are free and eventually turn pink. The sturdy stem is straight and slightly thicker at the base, smooth or fibrillose, and has the distinctive feature of staining blue when bruised or cut. The flesh is pale grey and smells faintly of radishes. The spores are pink.
HABITAT On decaying trunks and logs of deciduous trees, particularly willows and alders, especially near water. Summer to autumn.
EDIBILITY Not edible.

Yellow Shield
■ *Pluteus chrysophaeus*
Cap 3–5cm, height 5–10cm

DESCRIPTION Despite the species' common name, the hemispherical cap of the Yellow Shield is not always yellow, varying from lemon-coloured to light reddish brown, although it is usually yellow in the centre. The umbo is not always present. The cap surface is slightly wrinkled and the margin is lightly striated. The flesh is whitish or greyish and odourless. The gills are white to pinkish. The stem is slender and smooth, showing yellow or ochre patches with age. The spores are pink.
HABITAT On rotting broadleaf trees and buried wood. Summer to autumn.
POSSIBLE CONFUSION Very similar to the brown-capped Wrinkled Shield *Pluteus phlebophorus*, of which it is sometimes considered a variety, but that species is darker and has a more wrinkled cap.
EDIBILITY Not edible.

Stubble Rosegill

■ *Volvariella gloiocephala*
Cap 7–12cm, height 10–18cm

DESCRIPTION The genus *Volvariella* contains large fungi whose prominent volva persists into maturity. The cap of the Stubble Rosegill is ovoid, then conical and eventually flattened, with a central umbo. It is pale to mouse-grey, shiny in dry weather and viscous when wet. The gills are crowded, wide and free. The long white stem narrows at the top, darkening when old, and the base is enclosed in a large white volva. HABITAT Grows in open spaces rich in organic matter, including compost heaps. Summer and autumn, persisting as late as Dec.
EDIBILITY Edible but not good.

Piggyback Rosegill

■ *Volvariella surrecta*
Cap 3–7cm, height 6–9cm

SYNONYM *V. loveiana*.
DESCRIPTION One of the few parasitic gill fungi, and easily recognisable for this reason. The domed cap is pure white, smooth and velvety. The pink gills are free. The white stem is tall, fairly sturdy and ringless, but the prominent white volva is easily distinguishable since, as this is a parasitic fungus, it is not buried in the earth. The spores are pink.
HABITAT Parasitic, growing in large numbers on decaying specimens of the Clouded Funnel (p. 51), usually with more than 1 specimen per host fungus. Summer to late autumn.
EDIBILITY Not edible.

Pelargonium Webcap

■ *Cortinarius flexipes*
Cap 3–7cm, height 5–9cm

DESCRIPTION The webcaps (genus *Cortinarius*) are distinguished by a cobwebby partial veil, the cortina, which covers the gills completely in young specimens. The cap is conical, then flattened, with a central umbo; its surface is slightly fibrillose, and is dark grey in wet weather and paler when dry. Shreds of the white veil often hang from the pale margin. The brown or violet-brown flesh smells of geraniums. The gills are greyish with rust-brown and lilac shading. The long, slender stem is pale greyish brown, sometimes with a lilac tint at the top and ringed with white flakes from the centre downwards.

HABITAT Grows singly or in groups, under spruce and birch trees. Late summer to autumn.
EDIBILITY Not edible.

Stocking Webcap

■ *Cortinarius torvus*
Cap 5–10cm, height 6–9cm

DESCRIPTION The pale, brown, fleshy cap is hemispherical, then convex, and is covered in thin, dark brown, grey-brown or violet fibrils, especially towards the margin. The flesh of the cap is thick, violet at the top of the stem. The gills are thick and widely spaced, violet at first, then rust-coloured. The common name derives from the distinctive stem, which is white at the top but appears to be enclosed in a long, light brown to yellow sheath ending in a prominent ring, making it look as if it is wearing a stocking. The spores are rust-brown.

HABITAT Grows under Beech *Fagus sylvatica*. Autumn.
EDIBILITY **Poisonous**.

Birch Webcap

■ *Cortinarius triumphans*
Cap 8–15cm, height 10–15cm

DESCRIPTION The shiny, orange cap of
this large webcap is hemispherical, then
convex, with a wide central umbo. There is
a dark rim around the margin, the remains
of the veil. The gills are greyish white,
turning pale brown. The sturdy stem is
club-shaped or tapers to a point at the base,
where it is covered with white mycelium.
It is cloaked in the remains of the fugacious
veil in the form of a series of dark rings,
these turning rust-brown in older specimens
as they become covered with the spores.
HABITAT Grows in groups on damp soil
in parks and on lawns, in association with
birch trees. Autumn.
EDIBILITY **Poisonous**.

Red Banded Webcap

■ *Cortinarius armillatus*
Cap 6–10cm, height 10–17cm

DESCRIPTION The fleshy fawn cap is
covered in reddish down. It is bell-shaped
at first, then extended. The thin margin
eventually becomes upturned and may have
remains of the red veil hanging from it in
the form of small membranous fragments.
The gills are beige, turning rusty brown with
age. They are uneven in length, long and
short gills being interspersed, and are widely
spaced. The flesh is thick and pale brown.
The sturdy, cylindrical stem swells into a
bulb at the base. It is ringed with reddish-
orange filamentous bands that are sometimes
oblique, sometimes in a zigzag pattern.
HABITAT Under birch trees on damp
siliceous soil and in *Sphagnum* moss. Late
summer and autumn.
EDIBILITY **Poisonous**.

Variable Webcap

■ *Cortinarius anomalus* Cap 3–8cm, height 5–10cm

DESCRIPTION The ochre-brown or reddish cap flattens out, sometimes with a central umbo. The margin is regular when young, becoming wavy, is sometimes edged with violet, and has a few glistening scales. The flesh of the cap is pale violet, deeper in colour at the top of the stem. The crowded purple gills turn rusty brown from the spores. The stem, which thickens towards the base, is sometimes twice as long as the diameter of the cap and often slightly bent. It is bluish violet at the top and whitish or reddish at the base, and is banded with reddish fibrils that disappear with age.
HABITAT Grows in groups under birch and pine trees. Late summer to autumn.
EDIBILITY Not edible.

Scaly Webcap

■ *Cortinarius pholideus*
Cap 4–10cm, height 5–12cm

DESCRIPTION The pale brown cap of this distinctive mushroom is completely covered with tiny cinnamon-coloured squamules. The flesh is ochre-coloured, but violet in the top of the stem. The crowded gills are bluish violet at first, eventually turning rusty brown from the spores. The long, sturdy stem is sometimes bent. The lower two-thirds are covered with concentric rings of brown fibrils that are the same colour as the cap; from there to the underside of the cap, the stem is pale violet or brown and free of scales. The spores are rusty brown.
HABITAT In groups on peaty or very wet soil under birch trees or in mixed woods. Autumn.
EDIBILITY Not edible.

Violet Webcap
■ *Cortinarius violaceus*
Cap 5–12cm, height 6–12cm

DESCRIPTION This handsome mushroom
is easy to recognise owing to its all-purple
coloration and remains of the veil that
stick to the cap. The cap is hemispherical,
then concave, and has an even margin;
it has a velvety texture and darkens to
brown when old. The thick flesh of the
cap and stem is violet. The gills are thick
and widely spaced, darker than the cap
and stained with the rust-coloured spores
when mature. The stem, which is similar
in colour to the cap, swells at the base into
a spongy bulb.
HABITAT In damp deciduous forests. Late
summer and autumn.
EDIBILITY Edible, but turns the rest of the
food on the plate purple!

Dappled Webcap
■ *Cortinarius bolaris*
Cap 3–6cm, height 4–8cm

DESCRIPTION The cap is hemispherical
at first, then flattening, and is covered in
reddish scales against a yellow background.
The flesh is orange-yellow in the base of
the stem and white elsewhere, but turns
yellow when cut or bruised. The gills
are cream-coloured, becoming splashed
with rusty brown from the spores as the
fungus ages. The sturdy stem is yellow and
covered in rings of reddish scales that may
be regular or in a zigzag formation. The
base of the stem is sometimes covered in
the orange-red mycelium.
HABITAT In small groups on acid soil in
mixed woods or under deciduous trees,
especially oak, Beech *Fagus sylvatica* and
birch. Summer and autumn.
EDIBILITY Not edible; suspect.

Bloodred Webcap

■ *Cortinarius sanguineus*
Cap 2–5cm, height 4–7cm

SYNONYMS *C. puniceus, Dermocybe sanguinea.*
DESCRIPTION This large, handsome species is
entirely blood-red, including the flesh. The cap
is hemispherical at first, then flattening, with
a margin that becomes irregular and torn in
places. The cuticle is dry, slightly fibrillose at first,
becoming downy. The flesh is thin. The blood-red
gills are distant and uneven. The tough, narrow
stem thickens towards the base. It is covered in a
pale yellow or pink down when young.
HABITAT In colonies in mixed woods and under
conifers. Late summer and autumn.
POSSIBLE CONFUSION In the Surprise Webcap
C. semisanguineus, only the gills are blood-red
– the cap and stem are yellow. It is not edible
either.
EDIBILITY Not edible and suspect.

Brown Rollrim

■ *Paxillus involutus*
Cap 5–15cm, height 6–12cm

DESCRIPTION The rollrims have
the inrolled cap, crowded, decurrent
gills and short stem of a milkcap, but
they do not exude milk when cut
or bruised. All are poisonous. The
Brown Rollrim has a thick, fleshy
fawn to reddish-brown cap that
becomes depressed when older. It is
irregularly lobed and often eccentric.
The flesh is thick, soft and yellowish,
tending to turn reddish brown in
contact with the air. The gills are
cream-coloured at first, turning rusty
brown, are strongly decurrent and
are forked where they meet the cap; they can easily be separated from the cap.
The thick stem is pale brown under the cap, darker below. The spores are brown.
HABITAT Under broadleaf trees and conifers, in damp grassy places. Spring to autumn.
EDIBILITY **Poisonous**.

Oyster Rollrim

■ *Tapinella panuoides*
Cap 3–6cm, height 6–9cm

SYNONYM *Paxillus panuoides*.
DESCRIPTION The spatulate or fan-shaped cap has the typical inrolled margin of the genus, which in this species is smooth and sometimes undulating. The cuticle is velvety in texture, becoming leathery with age. It is yellowish brown to ochre and becomes paler in older specimens. The pale yellow gills are very decurrent and thin, wider where they are attached to the stem. The stem is very short; it is an extension of the fruiting body and is generally the same colour as the cap, although it is sometimes pale lilac at the base. HABITAT Grows on logs, trunks and branches of decaying conifers. Midsummer to early winter.
EDIBILITY **Poisonous**.

Velvet Rollrim

■ *Tapinella atrotomentosa*
Cap 10–25cm, height 4–8cm

SYNONYMS Blackbase Rollrim, *Paxillus atromentosus*.
DESCRIPTION The spatulate or fan-shaped cap is convex, then funnel-shaped or kidney-shaped, with an eccentric stem. The margin remains inrolled. The ochraceous or light brown cuticle is velvety in texture, cracking with age. The flesh is soft and spongy, white to pale yellow and brown in the stem. The cream to yellow gills turn brown when bruised or cut. They are decurrent, thin and branching where they are attached to the stem, and are easily separated from the cap. The stem is short and very thick, covered with a brownish-black down around the base. The spores are brown.
HABITAT Grows in tufts on conifer logs or roots. Summer to early autumn.
EDIBILITY **Poisonous**.

Common Rustgill

■ *Gymnopilus penetrans*
Cap 3–6cm, height 7–10cm

DESCRIPTION The bright orange-yellow
or russet cap is convex, then expands to
hemispherical. The cuticle is paler at the
edge. The flesh is whitish and has no smell.
The crowded gills are sulphur-yellow at first,
then rusty brown as they take on the colour of
the spores. The long stem is often incurving,
thickening at the bottom. It is whitish to
yellowish, covered in white fibrils, with traces
of a fugacious whitish ring (a remnant of the
partial veil, also possessed by this genus).
The base is surrounded by the fluffy white
mycelium.
HABITAT Grows in isolation or in tufts on
the rotting branches of conifers and on their
cones. Summer and autumn.
EDIBILITY **Poisonous**.

Spectacular Rustgill

■ *Gymnopilus junonius*
Cap 3–7cm, height 12–20cm

SYNONYMS Fiery Agaric, Laughing Jim,
G. *spectabilis*, *Pholiota spectabilis*.
DESCRIPTION The thick cap of this
spectacular mushroom is shallowly convex
when mature and sometimes umbonate. The
silky fibrous cuticle is reddish orange or fawn-
coloured, and the thick, firm flesh is yellow.
The bright rust-red gills are sinuate where
they meet the stem and darken when bruised
or cut. The fibrous stem is yellow above the
ring, darker below it. It is swollen or club-
shaped towards the base, and has a well-
marked membranous ring that is the same
fiery colour as the rest of the mushroom.
HABITAT On the stumps, branches or base
of broadleaf trees, especially oak. Summer to
autumn.
EDIBILITY **Poisonous** and hallucinogenic.

Poisonpie

■ *Hebeloma crustuliniforme*
Cap 5–10cm, height 5–10cm

DESCRIPTION The coffee-brown to fawn cap has a paler margin that is often wavy. It varies from hemispherical to flattened, with a shallow central umbo. The smooth cuticle becomes sticky in damp weather. The crowded, sinuate, cream-coloured gills darken with age, becoming rusty-brown when coloured with the ripe spores. The flesh is thick, white and smells strongly of radishes. The sturdy stem is straight and covered in small white floccules at the top. It is white.

HABITAT Grows in large groups in association with conifers and broadleaf trees; also found on heathland. Late summer to late autumn.

EDIBILITY **Poisonous**, though not as dangerous as the name implies.

Deadly Fibrecap

■ *Inocybe erubescens*
Cap 3–8cm, height 4–8cm

SYNONYMS Brick-red Tear Mushroom, Red-staining Inocybe, *I. patouillardii*.

DESCRIPTION The whitish to straw-coloured cap is conical, umbonate and fibrillose, becoming deeply cracked and split in older specimens. The cap, gills and stem all turn red when bruised or cut (a distinctive feature). The white flesh turns pinkish to red as it ages, especially in the stem. The gills are off-white, turning reddish with age. The tall, sturdy stem is white. The spores are brown.

HABITAT In well-lit woods, along paths, in clearings and in parks under broadleaf trees, especially lime. May–Jul.

EDIBILITY **Deadly poisonous**. All of the *Inocybe* species are inedible, and most are poisonous.

Split Fibrecap ▪ *Inocybe rimosa*
Cap 3–8cm, height 7–12cm

SYNONYM Silken-haired Inocybe, *Inocybe fastigiata*.

DESCRIPTION The straw-coloured, pale yellow or pale ochre cap is conical, with a large, pointed umbo. Its surface is very fibrillose and deeply split right up to the umbo in older specimens. The margin is incurved and irregular, and the flesh is white. The gills are yellowish green with a white edge, turning reddish with age. The tall, sturdy stem is white or pale ochre, covered in small, fluffy scales, especially at the top; it is often eccentric and incurving. The spores are brown.

HABITAT On well-drained sandy or limestone soil in coniferous and deciduous woods, on verges and in clearings. Summer and autumn.

EDIBILITY **Poisonous**.

White Fibrecap
▪ *Inocybe geophylla*
Cap 1–4cm, height 3–6cm

DESCRIPTION The white cap is conical with a large central umbo that is occasionally ochre in colour. The surface is smooth and silky, viscous when wet. The flesh is white or cream and has an unpleasant odour. The stem is white, swelling into a small bulb at the base, which is often covered in white mycelium. The crowded gills are off-white, beige or pale ochre, later darkening owing to the brown spores.

HABITAT Under deciduous trees, often in large numbers. Summer and autumn.

POSSIBLE CONFUSION The variety Lilac Fibrecap *I. geophylla* var. *lilacina* is entirely violet except for its umbo, which is brown; it could be confused with the edible Amethyst Deceiver (p. 55).

EDIBILITY **Deadly poisonous**.

Yellow Fieldcap

■ *Bolbitius titubans*
Cap 2–5cm, height 6–12cm

SYNONYMS *B. fragilis, B. vittellinus*.
DESCRIPTION The cap is egg-shaped at first,
expanding to a shallow hemisphere, when
the margin becomes cracked and deeply
furrowed. In young specimens the cap is
egg-yellow, but as it expands the yellow is
confined to the centre and the edges turn
white. The yellowish-white flesh is very thin.
The crowded gills are pale yellow, eventually
turning brown as they become covered
with mature spores. The stem is very straight and
tall in relation to the cap. It is white and
yellow, brittle and covered in tiny flakes.
HABITAT On rotting straw, compost, dung
and well-manured grass. Very fleeting,
having only a 24-hour lifespan. Spring to
autumn.
EDIBILITY Not edible.

Agrocybe rivulosa

Cap 3–12cm, height 8–12cm

DESCRIPTION The white to ochraceous,
wrinkled cap is egg-shaped at first, then
flattening to conical, with the margin
remaining inrolled. The flesh is thin and
whitish. The gills are crowded, greyish at
first, then turning brown from the brown
spores. The tall, sturdy, hollow stem is white
and thickens towards the base; it has a very
prominent fleshy, floppy white ring.
HABITAT This large mushroom is a
recent import, first recorded in northern
Europe (the Netherlands) in 2003, but has
spread rapidly since then. It originates in
subtropical and Mediterranean areas, so
prefers warm places. It lives on poplar and,
possibly, Beech *Fagus sylvatica* woodchips,
often in large groups. Summer to autumn.
EDIBILITY Unknown.

Sulphur Tuft

■ *Hypholoma fasciculare*
Cap 2–7cm, height 4–13cm

DESCRIPTION The smooth cap is globose at first, soon expanding to a shallow bowl shape. It is lemon-yellow at the margin, turning orange-brown towards the centre. The margin may have shreds of the yellow cortina hanging from it, and turns greenish grey when the fungus is mature. The gills are very thin and crowded, lemon-yellow at first, then darkening to olive-green as the spores ripen. A fugacious grey ring is sometimes visible two-thirds the way up the stem; the flesh in the stem is reddish.
HABITAT Grows in thick tufts on the dead logs and roots of coniferous and deciduous trees. Has a very long growing season, from spring to early winter.
EDIBILITY **Poisonous**.

Sheathed Woodtuft

■ *Kuehneromyces mutabilis*
Cap 3–8cm, height 4–10cm

SYNONYMS Changing Pholiota, *Pholiota mutabilis*.
DESCRIPTION The hygrophanous cap is honey-coloured in dry weather with an orange umbo, and reddish brown with a darker umbo when damp. It is convex at first, then expanding, with a marked central umbo. The margin is thin and translucent. The flesh of the cap is soft and cream-coloured. The gills are widely spaced and uneven, yellow at first and then rust-coloured from the spores. The stem is often curved; it is white and striated above the brown ring, yellow and scaly below it, and brown at the base.
HABITAT In large tufts on rotting Beech *Fagus sylvatica*, more rarely on conifers. Spring to summer.
EDIBILITY Edible except for the tough stem.

Golden Scalycap

■ *Pholiota aurivella*
Cap 7.5–10cm, height 6–12cm

DESCRIPTION The shiny, viscous cap is globose, then flattening. It is bright yellow, rust-coloured towards the centre, and is covered in chestnut-brown concentric scales or patches that are closer together towards the centre. The flesh is yellowish, red-brown in the base of the stem. The broad, adnate gills are pale yellow at first, then rust-coloured from the spores. The stem is yellow above the fugacious, scaly brown ring, and covered in chestnut-brown flat scales like those on the cap.

HABITAT At the base of tree trunks in clusters. Autumn.
POSSIBLE CONFUSION Often confused with the Shaggy Scalycap (p. 87), but the scales on that species are shaggy, not flat, and the cap is not slimy.
EDIBILITY Not edible.

Sticky Scalycap

■ *Pholiota gummosa*
Cap 3–6cm, height 6–10cm

DESCRIPTION The yellowish-green cap is egg-shaped at first, then flattening to hemispherical, with a ragged margin. It is extremely slimy, especially in young specimens and in wet weather, and is covered in small brown scales that are quite widely spaced apart. The flesh is cream or pale yellow. The pale yellow gills gradually turn reddish with age. The stem is long, often bent, and has more scales than the cap, except at the top above the fugacious ring, where it is smooth.

HABITAT In small clumps on wet clay soil, on the ground and on partially buried wood or logs. Summer and autumn.
POSSIBLE CONFUSION *P. spumosa* has a cap that drips with mucus, especially in wet weather, but it has no scales and is orange-yellow.
EDIBILITY Edible.

Shaggy Scalycap

■ *Pholiota squarrosa*
Cap 3–7cm, height 6–9cm

DESCRIPTION The pale yellow cap
and stem of this distinctive mushroom
are covered with erect reddish-brown
scales, arranged in concentric circles
that are denser towards the centre.
The margin remains inrolled for a long
time. The flesh is thick and fibrous, and
smells unpleasant. The pale yellow gills
are crowded and adnate, and turn rust-
coloured with age. The sinuous stem
narrows towards the base and is covered
in brown scales below the prominent
membranous ring, which is situated high
up, just below the cap; above the ring the
stem is smooth and yellow. Several stems
may grow together from the same point.
HABITAT Grows in dense tufts on conifers and broadleaf trees. Summer and autumn.
POSSIBLE CONFUSION Golden Scalycap (p. 86).
EDIBILITY Not edible.

Blue Roundhead

■ *Stropharia caerulea*
Cap 3–8cm, height 6–9cm

DESCRIPTION The cap is hemispherical,
then flattening, with a central umbo. It
is covered in a bluish-green mucus that
washes away as it matures, leaving it a
pale straw colour with a hint of green.
The margin is fringed with fine white
flakes. The flesh is pale blue-green. The
gills are buff-coloured, darkening to
brown when old. The narrow stem is the
same colour as the cap and the ring tends
to disappear. The spores are dark brown.
HABITAT On soil rich in organic
matter. Late summer to autumn.
POSSIBLE CONFUSION In the similar Verdigris Agaric *S. aeruginosa*, the cap and stem are
covered in white scales, these also forming a fringe on the margin, and the ring is persistent.
EDIBILITY Not edible.

Dung Roundhead

■ *Stropharia semiglobata*
Cap 2–4cm, height 5–10cm

DESCRIPTION The pale yellow or straw-coloured cap is globose, then hemispherical, and is silky when dry and viscous when wet. The whitish flesh is thin in the cap. The gills are broad, adnate and triangular in shape, and dark brown to blackish. The long, narrow stem is pale yellow, viscous, rigid and brittle; it is slightly swollen and darker yellow at the base, and ends in a bulb. There is a fugacious ring, quite low on the stem, which may not be evident, although it turns dark with age from the spores. The spores are blackish brown.
HABITAT On animal dung (mainly horse manure) in pastures. Late spring to autumn.
EDIBILITY Not edible.

Redlead Roundhead

■ *Leratiomyces ceres*
Cap 2–6cm, height 5–9cm

SYNONYMS *Hypholoma aurantiaca*, *Naematoloma aurantiaca*, *Stropharia aurantiaca*.
DESCRIPTION The cap is brick-red and convex, flattening to a shallow hemisphere. Remnants of the partial veil cling to the margin in young specimens. The surface is dry, but slimy when wet. The flesh is thin and whitish, pink under the cuticle. The crowded, adnexed to adnate gills are white to pale grey, darkening to purple-brown with white edges. The stem is white, smooth above the ring and with tiny scales below it; it stains orange as it ages, especially around the base, where it thickens. The white to orange ring occasionally disappears with age.
HABITAT Solitary or in groups on woodchips, occasionally in grass. Early autumn to late winter.
EDIBILITY Not edible.

Liberty Cap ■ *Psilocybe semilanceata*
Cap 1–2cm, height 5–12cm

SYNONYM Magic Mushroom.
DESCRIPTION The species' common name
derives from its resemblance to a Phrygian
bonnet, symbolic of liberty. The coffee-brown
to dirty-grey, yellowish or olive cap is conical
with a pointed umbo and it never flattens.
The margin is striated and stained black from
the spores in older specimens. The flesh is
pale brown and smells faintly of radishes. The
grey gills have a white edge and gradually
turn dark purplish brown with age. The very
long, thin, brittle stem is usually slightly
bent; it may be whitish or the same colour as
the cap, and is sometimes blue-green at the
base. The spores are dark brownish black.
HABITAT In groups on acid soil in damp
meadows. Late summer to late autumn.
EDIBILITY **Poisonous** and hallucinogenic.

Egghead Mottlegill
■ *Panaeolus semiovatus*
Cap 2–6cm, height 5–15cm

SYNONYM *P. separatus, Anellaria separata*.
DESCRIPTION The cap is bell-shaped
throughout its life, cream-coloured to
tan, silky and shiny, sticky when wet and
sometimes wrinkled; when dry, it often
cracks. The flesh is soft and whitish. The gills
are adnate, covered in a whitish veil when
young, free when mature. They are whitish
or grey when young, blackening when
mature. There is a thin ring, high up on the
brittle, slender white stem (this species is the
only member of the genus to have a ring, so
is classified separately by some authorities).
The ring is whitish, turning black from the
spores.
HABITAT On horse and cattle dung. Summer
and autumn.
EDIBILITY **Poisonous**.

Scaly Wood Mushroom

■ *Agaricus langei*
Cap 4–12cm, height 15–30cm

SYNONYM *Psalliota langei*.
DESCRIPTION The whitish cap of this large, handsome relative of the Cultivated Mushroom A. *bisporus* is covered in rust-coloured fibrils. The flesh is white, turning red when cut or bruised. The crowded, even gills are free, pink at first and turning purple-brown with age as the spores ripen. The sturdy stem is white, turning bright red when cut or bruised; it has a thick, floppy white ring. The spores are purplish black.

HABITAT On lime-rich soil, mainly in coniferous woods, although it is occasionally found in deciduous woodland. Summer and autumn.
POSSIBLE CONFUSION Easy to confuse with the Blushing Wood Mushroom A. *silvaticus*, whose scales are darker brown and more prominent, and which is also edible.
EDIBILITY Edible.

Field Mushroom

■ *Agaricus campestris*
Cap 5–12cm, height 3–8cm

SYNONYM *Psalliota campestris*.
DESCRIPTION The classic edible mushroom, closely related to the Cultivated Mushroom A. *bisporus*. It has a velvety white cap with a ragged margin that is easily peeled, revealing thick whitish flesh that turns pink when cut or bruised. In one variety, the cap may be covered in small brown scales. The crowded, even gills are pink in young specimens, turning greyish brown to purplish brown as the spores ripen. The thick white stem narrows slightly towards the base, and bears a thick, fleshy white ring.
HABITAT In fields, meadows and lawns. Found in large quantities after a long dry spell. Summer to early autumn.
EDIBILITY Edible and delicious; even safe to eat raw.

The Prince

▪ *Agaricus augustus*
Cap 8–15cm, height 8–15cm

SYNONYM *Psalliota augusta*.
DESCRIPTION The Prince has a pale yellow cap that is densely covered in concentric brown to reddish-brown scales that are closer together in the centre. It is globose at first, eventually flattening completely. The white flesh is thick and tender, smells of bitter almonds, and turns red on contact with the air, especially at the base of the stem. The crowded, even gills are pale pink in young specimens, later purplish brown. The thick white stem is covered in white scales or flakes; it has a thick double ring high up.
HABITAT In fields, meadows and lawns, parks and waste ground. Spring and autumn.
EDIBILITY Edible, although older specimens should be discarded.

Horse Mushroom

▪ *Agaricus arvensis*
Cap 15–20cm, height 8–12cm

SYNONYM *Psalliota arvensis*.
DESCRIPTION The cap is globose and white at first, turning ochre with age, especially in the centre. It may crack and appear scaly. The white flesh is thick and turns pale yellow when bruised; it smells of aniseed or bitter almonds. The crowded gills are pinkish grey, darkening to brownish black with a pale margin. The thick white stem may thicken or narrow towards the base; it has a thick double ring.
HABITAT In well-manured soil in grassland, parks and waste ground. Summer and autumn.
POSSIBLE CONFUSION May be mistaken for the only poisonous member of the genus, the Yellow Stainer A. *xanthodermus*, but that species stains bright yellow when cut or bruised and has an unpleasant smell.
EDIBILITY Edible.

Wood Mushroom

■ *Agaricus silvicola* Cap 7–14cm, height 5–12cm

SYNONYM *Psalliota sylvicola*.

DESCRIPTION The silky white cap is globose at first and then flattens to conical, sometimes becoming stained with yellow patches. The cuticle peels easily. The gills are very crowded and off-white at first, darkening to pinkish grey and then brownish black. The thick flesh is white. The tall, slender white stem ends in a bulb at the base; it has a floppy white ring and no volva.

HABITAT Grows in rings on humus-rich soil in mixed coniferous and deciduous woods. Summer and autumn.

POSSIBLE CONFUSION May be mistaken for the only poisonous member of the genus, the Yellow Stainer *A. xanthodermus*, but that species stains bright yellow when cut or bruised, and has an unpleasant smell and a thick, dentate double ring.

EDIBILITY Edible and good.

Weeping Widow

■ *Lacrymaria lacrymabunda* Cap 3–7cm, height 6–9cm

SYNONYMS *L. velutina, Psathyrella lacrimabunda*.

DESCRIPTION The cap is globose at first, flattening to conical with a distinct umbo as it ages, sometimes with ochre patches; it is covered in brown scales, especially at the margin, which give it a velvety appearance. The flesh is thin, firm and pale brown. The crowded gills 'weep' clear droplets, hence the species' common and scientific names. They are brown at first, edged with white, blackening as the spores mature. The stem is long and hollow; its white surface is covered in brown fibrils, especially at the base. Shreds of the cortina hang from the stem or margin.

HABITAT On grassland, in clumps, often with several stems growing from a single point. Autumn.

EDIBILITY Edible when young.

Brown Mottlegill
▪ *Panaeolina foenisecii*
Cap 2–3cm, height 4–7cm

SYNONYMS Brown Hay Cap, Haymaker, Mower's Mushroom, *Panaeolus foenisecii*.
DESCRIPTION The cap is convex, never completely flattening, with a finely striated margin. The cuticle is smooth or slightly granulose and reddish brown in damp weather, fading when dry. The flesh is thin and brown. The gills are thick, widely spaced and swollen. They are pale brown at first and mottled with the purple-brown spores when mature. The long, thin stem is hollow, covered in white flakes at the top, paler than the cap but reddening towards the base.
HABITAT This little fungus appears at the height of summer, at hay-making time, on lawns and pastures.
EDIBILITY **Poisonous**; probably hallucinogenic.

Pale Brittlestem
▪ *Psathyrella candolleana*
Cap 3–6cm, height 4–10cm

SYNONYM Crumble Tuft.
DESCRIPTION The cap is creamy white or ochre; it flattens completely when mature, with a tiny central umbo that is bright yellow. The remains of the white veil sometimes hang from the margin, which becomes ragged and turns black from the spores in old specimens. The thin flesh is greyish and waterlogged. The crowded gills are pinkish grey, then purplish brown from the spores. The long, slender white stem is hollow, brittle and striated at the top. The base is sometimes swollen into a bulb shape on which there are traces of the white mycelium.
HABITAT On rotten wood and on grass verges. From spring to autumn.
EDIBILITY Edible. Said to have hypoglycaemic properties.

Common Stump Brittlestem
■ *Psathyrella piluliformis* Cap 3–5cm, height 5–9cm

DESCRIPTION The cap is hygrophanous, ranging in colour from date-brown when waterlogged to pale ochre when dry. It is bell-shaped at first, expanding to hemispherical, and lacks an umbo. The remains of the veil sometimes hang from the margin. The thin

flesh is greyish. The gills are widely spaced, whitish at first, then turning cinnamon-brown and eventually purple-brown from the spores. The long, slender stem is hollow and brittle, white at the top and brown to ochre towards the base.
HABITAT Often grows in large tufts on logs or rotten wood. Summer and autumn.
POSSIBLE CONFUSION Conical Brittlestem (*below*) at its palest is similar.
EDIBILITY Edible. Said to have hypoglycaemic properties.

Conical Brittlestem
■ *Psathyrella conopilus* Cap 3–5cm, height 5–9cm

SYNONYMS Cone Brittlehead, *Parasola conopilus*.
DESCRIPTION The cap is conical and does not expand much over its lifetime. It is hygrophanous, ranging in colour from reddish brown when waterlogged to ochre when dry. There is an umbo the same colour as the cap, and the margin is finely striated. The thin flesh is greyish. The gills are widely spaced, white at first, then turning cinnamon-brown and eventually purple-brown from the spores. The long, slender stem is hollow and brittle. There is no ring.
HABITAT In woodland and parks, often in large tufts on rotten wood. Late spring to autumn.
POSSIBLE CONFUSION May be mistaken for other members of the genus *Psathyrella* and other small, conical fungi such as the Fairy Inkcap (p. 98).
EDIBILITY Not edible.

Shaggy Ink Cap

■ *Coprinus comatus*
Cap 2–6cm, height 10–20cm

SYNONYM Lawyer's Wig
DESCRIPTION This highly distinctive
mushroom has a tall, ovoid or conical cap
covered in shaggy white scales, except at the
top, where it is covered in a smooth brown
scale. As it matures, the margin turns black
from the spores and the whole cap gradually
dissolves into a sticky black mass, leaving only
the top of the cap and the stem. This process
is known as deliquescence. The gills are pink
at first, before turning black and liquefying.
The sturdy white stem is hollow, filled with a
cottony fibre; it has a thin white fugacious ring.
HABITAT Grassland. Apr to late autumn.
EDIBILITY Edible and delicious but only when
young, before it dissolves.

Magpie Inkcap

■ *Coprinus picaceus*
Cap 2–6cm, height 4–10cm

SYNONYM *Coprinopsis picacea*.
DESCRIPTION Similar in shape to the Shaggy
Ink Cap (above) and also deliquescent, but
shorter. It also grows from an egg shape, and
the black and white cap never expands. The
gills are off-white before they turn black and
liquefy. The whitish flesh has an unpleasant
gaseous or bituminous smell and tastes bitter.
The sturdy white stem is covered in small
white flakes and is hollow, filled with a cottony
fibre; there is a thin white fugacious ring.
HABITAT Grows in isolation or in groups in
forests, usually of Beech *Fagus sylvatica*, among
the fallen leaves. Prefers rich limestone soil.
Apr to late autumn.
POSSIBLE CONFUSION Firerug Inkcap
(p. 97).
EDIBILITY Not edible.

Common Inkcap

■ *Coprinus atramentarius*
Cap 3–7cm, height 5–15cm

SYNONYM *Coprinopsis atramentaria*.
DESCRIPTION Grows from a pale brown egg-shaped cap, which is darker at the top, striated and silky, and expands into an umbrella shape. The gills are off-white before they turn black and liquefy. The margin becomes ragged as the fungus begins to deliquesce. The thin brown flesh has a pleasant taste and smell. The sturdy, hollow white stem is slightly swollen just below the cap.
HABITAT Grows in dense tufts, stuck together or welded at the base of the stem, on rotting wood in grassland. Summer to autumn.
EDIBILITY Not edible. Particularly nasty effects if consumed with alcohol. It was once used in aversion therapy to treat alcoholics. The liquefied cap and gills have been used as ink.

Snowy Inkcap

■ *Coprinus niveus*
Cap 1–3cm, height 4–8cm

SYNONYM *Coprinopsis nivea*.
DESCRIPTION A pure white mushroom that is typically egg-shaped when young. Later, it expands to become bell-shaped, sometimes opening out like an umbrella and occasionally splitting at the margin. The off-white cap is covered in tiny powdery scales like a dusting of snow, which are the remnants of the veil. The long, crowded white gills soon turn grey, then black and they deliquesce. The thin brown flesh has a neutral taste and no smell. The tall, hollow white stem is brittle and thickly covered in cottony flakes, especially at the base. The spores are black.
HABITAT In grassland, on cow-pats, horse manure and rotting straw. May–Nov.
EDIBILITY Not edible.

Glistening Inkcap

■ *Coprinellus micaceus*
Cap 3–5cm, height 2–4cm

SYNONYM *Coprinus micaceus*.
DESCRIPTION The cap is pale brown, deeper
brown in the centre, and is distinguished by
having a few shiny specks on the top that
glisten like mica. It is bell-shaped and covered
in deep, narrow furrows. The crowded gills are
greyish white before turning brown. They are
sometimes, but not always, deliquescent. The
thin white silky stem is sometimes decorated
with a black fugacious ring.
HABITAT Grows in thick tufts on rotting wood
in woodland.
POSSIBLE CONFUSION The Hare's-foot
Inkcap C. *lagopus* (*Coprinopsis lagopus*) is
similar, with a greyish to silver partial coating
of scales on its pleated brown cap; its stem is
covered in down and has no ring.
EDIBILITY Not edible.

Firerug Inkcap

■ *Coprinellus domesticus*
Cap 3–7cm, height 6–9cm

SYNONYM *Coprinus domesticus*.
DESCRIPTION Has the typical inkcap shape.
The brown cap is covered in thick flakes, the
remnants of the veil, and becomes deeply
striated as it expands. The crowded, free
gills turn brown, then black. The white stem
is thicker than in most inkcaps. The most
distinctive feature is the thick mesh of orange
mycelium at the base of the stem, known as an
ozonium, which spreads around it.
HABITAT On all types of dead wood.
Occasionally found indoors, growing on rafters
and waterlogged carpets; here, the ozonium is
less prominent or absent. Spring to autumn.
POSSIBLE CONFUSION Similar to Magpie
Inkcap (p. 95), but the cuticle of Firerug Inkcap is paler.
EDIBILITY Not edible.

Fairy Inkcap ■ *Coprinellus disseminatus*
Cap 1–2cm, height 2–5cm

SYNONYM Fairy's Bonnet, *Coprinus disseminatus*, *Psathyrella disseminata*.
DESCRIPTION The deeply pleated cap of this tiny fungus is ovoid at first, expanding to bell-shaped, and has a woolly mouse-grey surface with a central brown spot. The brown flesh is so thin that it is almost invisible. The white gills are adnate, and each furrow in the cap corresponds to a gill. Unlike other inkcaps, it is not deliquescent; the margin merely becomes ragged and the gills turn black when old.
HABITAT In grassy places and on old tree stumps. Grows in huge numbers of many hundreds of specimens. Summer and autumn.
POSSIBLE CONFUSION Similar to Pleated Inkcap (*below*), but that species does not grow in such large numbers.
EDIBILITY Not edible.

Pleated Inkcap ■ *Coprinopsis plicatilis*
Cap 2–3cm, height 4–7cm

SYNONYM *Coprinus plicatilis*, *Parasola plicatilis*.
DESCRIPTION This tiny inkcap looks like a parasol when expanded, with its greyish cap regularly covered in deep, narrow furrows. It has a clearly defined central beige disc, surrounded by a white circle that is not furrowed. The grey gills turn black and ragged when mature but do not deliquesce. The dark flesh is extremely thin and fragile. The tall, hollow stem is white and translucent, often with a small bulb at the base. The spores are black. Some authorities have reclassified this species and other black-spored fungi that do not deliquesce and whose caps expand into a new genus, *Parasola*.
HABITAT Grows in isolation or with 1 or 2 others on fertile grassland, lawns or at roadsides.
POSSIBLE CONFUSION Fairy Inkcap (*above*).
EDIBILITY Not edible.

Oyster Mushroom

■ *Pleurotus ostreatus*
Cap 8–20cm, height 2–5cm

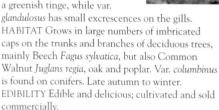

DESCRIPTION The smooth grey, greyish-brown or greyish-violet cap is shell-shaped or fan-shaped and the margin remains incurved. The flesh is thick at the centre of the cap and white. The crowded white decurrent gills converge towards the eccentric stem. The short white stem is lateral, eccentric or virtually non-existent. The spores are white. In the variety var. *columbinus*, the cap has a greenish tinge, while var. *glandulosus* has small excrescences on the gills.
HABITAT Grows in large numbers of imbricated caps on the trunks and branches of deciduous trees, mainly Beech *Fagus sylvatica*, but also Common Walnut *Juglans regia*, oak and poplar. Var. *columbinus* is found on conifers. Late autumn to winter.
EDIBILITY Edible and delicious; cultivated and sold commercially.

Branching Oyster

■ *Pleurotus cornucopiae*
Cap 4–15cm, height 4–10cm

DESCRIPTION The elegant, vase-shaped caps may be beige, cream-coloured or various shades of light brown. The cap is flat at first, becoming funnel-shaped, and the margin is initially thin and inrolled or incurved. The flesh is white with a strong smell of meal. The crowded white or cream gills are deeply decurrent, ending in a ridge on the stem. The cream or white stem is thick and curved, and narrows towards the base.
HABITAT In large tufts on dying or dead broadleaf trees, especially elms. Spring to autumn.
EDIBILITY Edible and delicious; cultivated and sold commercially.

Veiled Oyster ▪ *Pleurotus dryinus*
Cap 6–15cm, height 3–5cm

SYNONYM Oak Oyster.

DESCRIPTION The greyish or off-white cap is almost circular and the outline of the mature fungus is shaped like a plate, making it look more like a bracket fungus than an oyster mushroom. The margin may have wisps of the white veil hanging from it. The cap is covered in whitish felty scales when young, but these disappear in the adult specimen. The flesh is thick and white. The crowded white gills are deeply decurrent. The short, thick stem is completely eccentric, very tough and deeply embedded in the substrate.

HABITAT On the trunks and branches of many deciduous trees, especially oak, very occasionally on pines. Autumn.

EDIBILITY Edible when young.

Splitgill
▪ *Schizophyllum commune*
Cap 1–3.5cm, height 1–2cm

SYNONYM Common Porecrust.

DESCRIPTION The leathery fan-shaped brackets are often lobed or fused at the base with other brackets. The upper surface is densely covered in erect grey-brown hairs, which are paler when the fungus is dry. The under surface consists of widely spaced gills that are split lengthways. The tough flesh is thin and grey-brown. The eccentric stem may be completely absent. The spores are white.

HABITAT Grows in tufts or groups on all types of wood, on ferns and even on straw, fruiting after rainfall. It is said to be the most widespread fungus in the world, growing on every continent except Antarctica. Year-round.

EDIBILITY Not edible.

Peeling Oysterling
■ *Crepidotus mollis* Cap 2–7cm

DESCRIPTION The hygrophanous, scaly cap, which is whitish or beige in dry weather and ochre to brownish grey when wet, is fan- or kidney-shaped. The surface is covered with a detachable layer of slime in younger specimens, which may wash away after heavy rain. The flesh has a gelatinous consistency. The gills are crowded and white, turning brown with age, and radiate from the point at which the cap is attached to the tree. The spores are brown.

HABITAT In groups and tufts on dead wood, logs or fallen branches of broadleaf trees. Year-round.

POSSIBLE CONFUSION The Variable Oysterling (*below*) is similar but smaller, and is often pure white.

EDIBILITY Not edible.

Variable Oysterling
■ *Crepidotus variabilis* Cap 0.5–3cm

DESCRIPTION The kidney- or fan-shaped cap is a brilliant white, and is often attached directly to the substrate without a stem. The flesh is thin, white and odourless. The gills are distant and of uneven length, radiating in a fan shape from the point at which the cap is attached. They are white or cream at first, turning cinnamon-brown. The spores are brown.

HABITAT Grows along branches and twigs of broadleaf trees, and it can fruit on log piles or bunches of twigs in damp places. Mostly summer and autumn, but can be found year-round during mild winters.

POSSIBLE CONFUSION Peeling Oysterling (*above*).

EDIBILITY Not edible.

Scurfy Twiglet
■ *Tubaria furfuracea*
Cap 3–7cm, height 5–6cm

DESCRIPTION The cap is hygrophanous, changing from cinnamon-brown when moist to pale tan when dry. The surface is covered in tiny flakes and the margin bears remnants of the white veil. The cap is convex at first, then flattening completely. The margin is striate when moist. The flesh is pale brown. The gills are brown, broadly adnate or slightly decurrent. The slender, tall, hollow stem is the same colour as the cap or deeper brown, and scaly when young; the base is surrounded by a fluffy white mycelium. The spores are yellowish brown.
HABITAT On the ground in woods and in grass. Mainly in autumn to early winter but may grow throughout the year.
EDIBILITY Not edible.

Rosy Spike
■ *Gomphidius roseus*
Cap 3–6cm, height 3–6cm

DESCRIPTION The members of the genus *Gomphidius* have a distinctive silhouette. The cap and stem merge into each other in one piece, as can be seen if a specimen is sliced vertically. The gills are small and decurrent, and the cap is small in relation to the height of the mushroom. The Rosy Spike has a brilliant, slimy, red or pink cap that is convex at first, then flattening but remaining hemispherical. The flesh is whitish, but red under the cuticle. The gills are widely spaced and decurrent, white at first, then turning grey.
HABITAT Under pine trees and in clearings, often found growing with the Bovine Bolete (p. 23). Summer and autumn.
EDIBILITY Not edible.

Copper Spike
■ *Chroogomphus rutilus*
Cap 5–10cm, height 6–13cm

SYNONYM *Gomphidius viscidus*.
DESCRIPTION Has the typical conical,
then hemispherical, cap of the genus. The
wide, decurrent gills are barely covered by
the slimy copper-coloured, reddish-brown
or puce cap, which is perched on top
of the gills like a little hat. The margin
remains inrolled for a long time. The flesh
is orange-red, tending to darken when cut
or bruised. The gills are reddish ochre,
turning dark brown with age. The reddish
stem, which is covered in small red scales,
narrows towards the top and is sometimes
swollen in the centre.
HABITAT Under conifers, mainly pines,
sometimes under solitary trees or in
hedgerows. Late summer and autumn.
EDIBILITY Not edible.

Chanterelle ■ *Cantharellus cibarius*
Cap 3–10cm, height 4–5cm

DESCRIPTION The species of this genus
have veins or ribs in place of true gills.
The Chanterelle is easy to spot owing
to its brilliant yellow colour. The cap
and stem are all of a piece. The margin
is very wavy and becomes funnel-shaped
when older. The stem is short, narrowing
towards the base, and the thick flesh is
white, as are the spores.
HABITAT Grows in large numbers under
broadleaf trees and conifers after rain.
Jun–Oct.
POSSIBLE CONFUSION The mushroom
most closely resembling the Chanterelle
is the False Chanterelle (p. 105), which
has true gills; it is not good to eat, and is
considered by some to be poisonous.
EDIBILITY Edible and delicious.

Trumpet Chanterelle

■ *Cantharellus tubaeformis*
Cap 2–7cm, height 2–8cm

DESCRIPTION Has a small, wavy cap at the top of a long, fairly thick stem. The cap is ochre to brownish grey, with a central depression becoming funnel-shaped in older specimens. The underside of the cap is ochre or golden yellow, and has folds or ribs that are decurrent and widely spaced. The sinuous stem, which is occasionally ribbed, is the same colour as the underside of the cap; it is often quite thick. The flesh is thin and elastic, with a faintly pleasant taste and smell.

HABITAT Grows in tightly packed clumps on moss and pine-needle litter in coniferous forests, but also found under Beech *Fagus sylvatica*. Sep–Dec.
EDIBILITY Edible, but has a rubbery consistency.

Horn of Plenty

■ *Craterellus cornucopioides*
Height 3–10cm

SYNONYMS Black Chanterelle, Black Trumpet, Trumpet of the Dead.
DESCRIPTION Despite its sinister name and appearance, the Horn of Plenty makes excellent eating. It consists of a hollow funnel or trumpet shape with a thick, outward-curving lip and black interior. The grey exterior of the funnel is downy, smooth or slightly veined, and may blacken when wet. The flesh is thin and elastic. The sinuous stem narrows at the base. The spores are white. As the fungus ages, it tends to deliquesce, and the pleasant, fruity smell becomes unpleasant.
HABITAT Found in large numbers under broadleaf trees, and under spruces at high altitude; prefers clay and limestone soils. Jun to early winter.
EDIBILITY Edible and delicious when young.

False Chanterelle
■ *Hygrophoropsis aurantiaca*
Cap 3–7cm, height 3–10cm

SYNONYM *Clitocybe aurantiaca*.
DESCRIPTION The cap is convex
at first but soon develops a central
depression, and the wavy margin is
inrolled for a long time. The colour
is orange to yellow, sometimes darker
in the centre. The whitish flesh is soft
and elastic. The orange-red to pale
yellow gills are crowded, decurrent
and often forked. The thin, smooth,
fibrous stem is narrower at the base
and hollow at first; it is reddish, a
darker shade than the cap. The spores
are white.

HABITAT In small groups on the ground or on rotting wood in coniferous forests, mainly
pine and spruce. Late summer and autumn.
EDIBILITY Edible, but not good and considered poisonous by some.

Dryad's Saddle
■ *Polyporus squamosus*
Cap 20–70cm

SYNONYM *Melanopus squamosus*.
DESCRIPTION Like all polypores,
Dryad's Saddle has a small or non-
existent lateral stem that anchors it to
the tree on which it grows. The large
caps are imbricated, growing on top of
each other to create large tufts. The
cap is kidney-shaped and covered in
concentric scales that range in colour
from reddish brown to dark ochre on
a smooth, beige to ochre background.
The cream-coloured underside of the
cap is covered in wide, angular, ragged
tubes ending in pores. The flesh is
firm when young, leathery in older
specimens.

HABITAT Grows on deciduous trees, mainly oaks. Spring and summer.
EDIBILITY Edible only when young, before it becomes too tough to cook.

Blackfoot Polypore
■ *Polyporus leptocephalus* Cap 3–12cm

SYNONYMS *P. elegans*, *P. varius*, *Melanopus varius*.

DESCRIPTION The cap is leathery and pale ochre brown, hence the fungus's scientific name, *leptocephalus*, meaning 'hare's head'. It is highly irregular and lobed, flattened or curving, depressed in the centre and often raised at the sides. The texture is smooth and velvety. The flesh is brown, thin and fibrous. The tubes are very short, ending in small pores that are off-white or pale yellow. The short stem is equally tough in consistency and is either lateral or eccentric; it is divided crossways into 2 clearly defined halves, white at the top and black at the base, hence the species' common name.
HABITAT On logs and the trunks of dead broadleaf trees. Summer and autumn.
EDIBILITY Not edible.

Tuberous Polypore
■ *Polyporus tuberaster*
Cap 5–15cm, height 2–3cm

SYNONYM *P. forquignonii*.
DESCRIPTION This fungus has a very varied appearance. The circular cap has an inrolled margin and is covered in tiny, erect coffee-coloured scales on a whitish or pale brown background. The flesh is white. The pores on the underside of the cap are strongly decurrent and whitish, then cream and finally yellowish. The stem may be central or eccentric and is sturdy when young, widening considerably at the top. It is whitish, but ochraceous at the base. The spores are also white.
HABITAT On logs and the trunks of dead broadleaf trees, as well as on wood buried in the ground. Spring to late summer.
EDIBILITY Edible but tough.

Hairy Curtain Crust
▪ *Stereum hirsutum* Cap 2–5cm

DESCRIPTION In the early stages of its development, the fungus forms a crust over the wood on which it grows. This develops into superimposed caps that are welded together to form large masses (the measurement above is for a single cap). The upper surface of the caps is downy, even hirsute, and ringed with concentric circles of various colours, including brown, rust-red and orange; they are often edged with white, especially at the margin, and the colour is darker where the cap is attached to the substrate. The underside is smooth, orange-yellow at first and then ochre. The margin is undulating and lobed, bright yellow in young specimens. The flesh and spores are white.

HABITAT On dead trees. Year-round.
EDIBILITY Not edible.

Bleeding Oak Crust
▪ *Stereum gausapatum* Cap 2–5cm

SYNONYM *S. spadiceum*.
DESCRIPTION As in the Hairy Curtain Crust (above), individual specimens of this fungus are attached to each other, forming large masses. The upper surface of the caps is downy and velvety, coloured in concentric circles of various shades of brown. The margin is undulating and lobed, white in young specimens. The white flesh is thin, soft and flexible when fresh, and the spores are white. The fungus bleeds red droplets when cut or bruised.

HABITAT On deciduous trees, especially oaks. It can be both saprophytic and parasitic, its rhizomorphs attacking the heartwood and producing long channels of rot. Year-round.
POSSIBLE CONFUSION Turkeytail (p. 123), but that species does not exude red droplets.
EDIBILITY Not edible.

Bleeding Conifer Crust

■ *Stereum sanguinolentum* Cap 2–5cm

DESCRIPTION The fungus first forms round patches when young, sometimes with a reversed margin forming a cap. Eventually, it breaks away from the wood on which it grows to form a mass of lobed, imbricated caps. Their upper surface is smooth, with radiating fibrils; it is fawn-coloured and ringed in concentric circles, usually with a wide orange margin tipped with white that is undulating and lobed. The white flesh is thin. The underside of the cap is dirty white or buff, bleeding red droplets when cut or bruised.
HABITAT Only on conifers, on which it is a dangerous parasite. Year-round.
EDIBILITY Not edible.

Moor Club ■ *Clavaria argillacea* Height 2–5cm

DESCRIPTION The fairy clubs are a group of Aphyllophoroid fungi whose spore-bearing hymenium covers the body of the fungus. They vary in shape from thick and truncated

to antler-like, and are generally rather small. The Moor Club grows as a group of tall, pale yellow or greenish-yellow stalks on a stem that is distinct and of a deeper colour. The flesh is fibrous. The spores are white, cream or yellow.
HABITAT Heaths and moors. Summer to autumn.
POSSIBLE CONFUSION The Yellow Club (p. 110) grows in heathland and is also yellow, but is taller and more brightly coloured. May also be confused with Golden Spindles (p. 109).
EDIBILITY Not edible and suspect.

White Spindles

■ *Clavaria fragilis* Height 2–5cm

DESCRIPTION The thin, matt white stalks of this fairy club are translucent, smooth and fragile, narrowing at the top. They may also curve or bend at the top but are mostly straight. The spore-bearing hymenium covering the stalks is white, as are the spores. The stems may be welded together at the base.

HABITAT Like most fairy clubs, White Spindles grows on bare ground or in the grass of fields, gardens and parks, sometimes in large clumps. Late summer to winter.

EDIBILITY Not edible and suspect.

Golden Spindles

■ *Clavulinopsis fusiformis*
Height 5–15cm, width <1.5cm

SYNONYM *Clavaria fusiformis*.
DESCRIPTION The smooth, bright yellow stalks may vary in colour from lemon- to saffron-yellow. They are sometimes branched and joined at the base, and occasionally appear to be grooved vertically where 2 stalks have fused together. The base of the stem is white, as are the spores. The flesh is thin and yellow.

HABITAT In the grass under broadleaf trees or conifers. Summer and autumn.

POSSIBLE CONFUSION Similar to the much smaller Moor Club (p. 108) and the Yellow Club (p. 110), but differs from both in the bitter taste of its flesh.

EDIBILITY Not edible.

Yellow Club

■ *Clavulinopsis helvola*
Height 7cm, width <0.4cm

SYNONYM *Clavaria helvola*.
DESCRIPTION The tall, narrow stalks are
often bent and twisted like so many upright
worms. They are sometimes branched
and joined at the base, ending in a barely
separable stem. The colour varies from
golden yellow to apricot. The flesh is thin
and yellow. The spores are white.
HABITAT In moss in forests and among
heather. Summer and autumn.
POSSIBLE CONFUSION Similar to the
smaller but more robust Moor Club
(p. 108), and to Golden Spindles (p. 109),
which is larger and thicker.
EDIBILITY Not edible.

Meadow Coral

■ *Clavulinopsis corniculata*
Height 2.5–3cm

SYNONYMS *Clavaria corniculata*,
Ramariopsis corniculata.
DESCRIPTION This tiny fairy club is bright
egg-yellow, orange or ochre like some
specimens of Yellow Club (*above*), but the
slender branches are divided into 2 or 3
sub-branches with blunt, rounded tips like
corals or antlers. The flesh is pale yellow
and has a mealy odour and taste. The
stem may be absent, or if present is very
short, downy at the base and covered in
the white mycelium. The spores are white.
The variety known as var. *pratensis* has very
crowded branches of equal length that are
level at the top.
HABITAT On grassland in parks, gardens
and mossy meadows, growing alone or in
clumps; also found under coniferous or
broadleaf trees. Autumn.
EDIBILITY Not edible.

Giant Club ■ *Clavariadelphus pistillaris*
Height 8–20cm, width 2–6cm

SYNONYM Giant Fairy Club, *Clavaria pistillaris*.
DESCRIPTION The tall, narrow stalks of this
truly club-shaped club fungus, which widen
at the top and look as if they might be deadly
weapons if they were bigger and heavier,
vary in colour from orange to ochre or bright
yellow. The white flesh has a bitter taste.
HABITAT Under broadleaf trees, mostly in
Beech *Fagus sylvatica* woods. Summer and
autumn.
POSSIBLE CONFUSION The Club Coral
C. truncatus is similar, but is a deeper yellow
and looks as if someone has sliced off the top.
It grows under conifers on limestone soil and
has sweeter flesh, so it is edible.
EDIBILITY Not edible.

Crested Coral
■ *Clavulina coralloides*
Height 2.5–8cm

SYNONYMS White Coral
Fungus, *Clavaria coralloides*.
DESCRIPTION The dense
clumps of this white or pale
yellow fungus branch profusely
from 1 or more thick stems
into crested tips or ragged
edges. It is often parasitised by
the mould *Helminthosphaeria
clavarium* from the base
upwards, changing the colour
to grey or black and making it
look more like the Grey Coral
Clavaria cinerea, but the black

dots of the mould are visible under a magnifying glass.
HABITAT On the ground, under broadleaf trees and conifers. Summer and autumn.
POSSIBLE CONFUSION If parasitised, it may resemble the Cinder Coral (see 'Description').
The taller White Crested Coral has the same habitat and is now considered to be a variety
of the Crested Coral.
EDIBILITY Not edible.

Rosso Coral
■ *Ramaria botrytis* Height 10–20cm

DESCRIPTION This very massive fairy club grows in large clumps that may be up to 20cm in diameter. The thick white trunk branches extensively like a broadleaf tree, ending in rounded or pointed, branched pink to wine-red tips. The flesh is greyish white, pinkish at the very tip. It has a pleasant taste and smell. The spores are white. The species has several varieties, including var. *panula*, which is very small with pink-tipped branches; var. *alba*, which is all white; and var. *musaecolor*, which has a yellow trunk and branches.
HABITAT Grows in thick clumps in dense forests of Beech *Fagus sylvatica* and conifers. Summer and autumn.
EDIBILITY Edible; sought after in some parts of France.

Upright Coral
■ *Ramaria stricta*
Height 7–15cm, width 7–10cm

DESCRIPTION Has tall, upright branches that are tightly packed in clumps growing from short, parallel, branching trunks. It is cinnamon-coloured or ochre-brown all over, with yellowish tips. The flesh is bitter. The spores are white. All parts bruise wine red.
HABITAT One of the few fairy clubs that grows on wood, favouring rotting conifers and broadleaf trees. Spring to autumn.
POSSIBLE CONFUSION *R. abietina* (p. 113) is very similar in shape and has a similar habitat, but is greenish yellow in colour. The flesh is not bitter but the fungus is considered to be of no interest as a food.
EDIBILITY Not edible.

Bracken Club
■ *Typhula quisquiliaris* Height 3–5mm

DESCRIPTION This charming and distinctive little fungus appears as tiny white clubs that grow in rows along the dead stems of Bracken. The clubs themselves have a short and distinct stem and a rounded to pear-shaped head. Unsurprisingly, the species is easiest to find in early winter when Bracken stems are waterlogged and decaying.

HABITAT Widespread and found mostly in woodland with a dense growth of Bracken, but sometimes also occurs in open, heathy areas, in locations where this invasive fern forms extensive stands. Autumn and winter.

EDIBILITY Not edible.

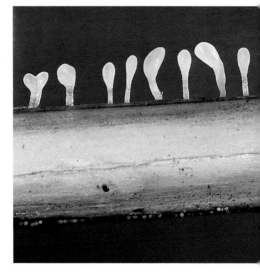

Wood Cauliflower
■ *Sparassis crispa* Diameter <40cm

DESCRIPTION This handsome, distinctive fungus looks like a large yellow frisée or Batavia lettuce. It grows from a single stem, branching into numerous flattened, incurving whitish or yellowish lobed branches with ragged edges, which are the hymenium for the white spores.

HABITAT Usually grows in isolation at the base of pine trees, where it forms mycorrhiza with the roots. Summer and autumn.

POSSIBLE CONFUSION The only other related species (considered by some authorities to be a variety of

S. crispa) is *S. laminosa*, also known as *S. brevipes*, which prefers oak trees. Its branches are more flattened and translucent, resembling a yellowish sea lettuce. It has a slightly spicy smell, which is sometimes unpleasant, and it is also edible.

EDIBILITY Edible and delicious, but requires careful cleaning.

Stinkhorn ■ *Phallus impudicus*
Cap 4–5cm, height 15–20cm

SYNONYM *Ithyphallus impudicus*.
DESCRIPTION An unmistakable fungus,
but for the reasons that its name implies. It grows
from an off-white 'egg', which, when cut open, reveals
a greenish jelly surrounding what will eventually
become the cap. If the fungus is allowed to sprout out
of the 'egg', it shoots up overnight on a white to off-
white spongy stalk topped by a globose, reticulated
cap, which is totally covered in a greenish slime that
gives off an appalling odour, comparable to that of
rotting flesh. This attracts swarms of flies that eat
away the slime to reveal the spongy, hollow, pale
yellow cap.
HABITAT Among humus. Summer and autumn.
EDIBILITY Not edible.

Dog Stinkhorn
■ *Mutinus caninus*
Cap 0.5cm, height 7–10cm

DESCRIPTION Grows from a more
oblong 'egg' than the Stinkhorn (*above*),
which like that species is attached to
white mycelial cords. Inside the 'egg',
the stem and cap are orange. The stem,
which is often curved, emerges quickly
as the fungus develops; it is pale yellow
or off-white. The spongy, reticulated
cap is covered in a thick blackish slime,
beneath which there is a spongy, bright
orange cap. The smell is unbearable.
HABITAT On damp humus in shaded
forests, sometimes on rotting wood.
Summer and autumn.
POSSIBLE CONFUSION Related species
include the Veiled or Netted Stinkhorn
Dictyophora duplicata; this has a long
white veil hanging from the dark, slimy
cap, the latter topped with a small white
lump.
EDIBILITY Not edible.

Small Stagshorn

■ *Calocera cornea*
Height 1–2cm, width 0.5–2mm

DESCRIPTION The stagshorns are like miniature versions of coral fungi, but their flesh is of a different consistency. They are not edible owing to their small size. This tiny yellow-orange species is smooth or longitudinally striated, and cylindrical or tongue-shaped. The tip is pointed, occasionally forked. The stem is not separate from the spore-bearing hymenium. The flesh, as in all stagshorns, is cartilaginous and elastic.

HABITAT Usually on the dead wood of deciduous trees, singly or in clumps. Summer and autumn.

POSSIBLE CONFUSION The Forked Stagshorn C. *furcata* looks similar but grows on pine trees.

EDIBILITY Not edible.

Yellow Stagshorn

■ *Calocera viscosa* Height 3–8cm

DESCRIPTION This stagshorn looks like a tiny tree. It is mainly yellow, but the tips of the deeply forked branches are orange. The surface is smooth and has a slimy or greasy texture, making it hard to grasp the fungus, which tends to slide out of your fingers if you attempt to pick it, especially as the stem is deeply embedded in the substrate. The flesh is soft and elastic.

HABITAT On the rotten wood of dead conifers. Summer and autumn.

POSSIBLE CONFUSION The Forked Stagshorn C. *furcata* looks similar and also grows on pine trees, but it consists of many individual jelly-like yellowish-brown stalks with only occasional branches. There is also a possibility of confusion with the yellow fairy clubs (pp. 108–13), but these are larger with thicker, trunk-like stems.

EDIBILITY Not edible.

Witches' Butter

■ *Exidia glandulosa*
Diameter 1–6cm, thickness 1–3cm

DESCRIPTION This quaintly named but highly unprepossessing fungus is one of the so-called jelly fungi that are very variable in shape but entirely gelatinous in texture. Witches' Butter looks like a shiny lump of dark brown to black animal excrement. It may be lumpy or folded, resembling brain tissue. The flesh is gelatinous, shrinking and swelling, depending on the weather. The underside, the spore-bearing hymenium, is covered in conical warts. The spores are white.
HABITAT Grows on the branches of dead broadleaf trees, especially oak, sometimes in large numbers. Spring to autumn.
EDIBILITY Not edible.

Cowberry Redleaf

■ *Exobasidium vaccinii* Microscopic

DESCRIPTION This is one of the few basidiomycetes that is a microscopic mould rather than a large fruiting body. As its common name implies, the species mainly attacks the Cowberry *Vaccinium vitis-idaea* (also known variously as Lingonberry, Foxberry, Mountain Cranberry and Red Whortleberry), whose bright red fruits are similar to cranberries. It also occasionally attacks plants of the same genus, such as bilberries and blueberries. The mould appears on the green leaves, producing bright to dark red patches or galls. As the fungus matures and forms its mealy white spore-bearing hymenium, it causes the leaves to shrivel and die.
HABITAT Green leaves of plants of the genus *Vaccinium*. Appears in summer and autumn.
EDIBILITY Not edible.

Hen of the Woods
■ *Grifola frondosa*
Cap 10–20cm

SYNONYMS Tufted Polypore, *Polyporus frondosus*.
DESCRIPTION Consists of a mass of branching white stems that are often welded together at the base, terminating in flattish, depressed and umbelliferous caps, which may be yellow-brown or grey. The cap is smooth and velvety, and is covered in short, rough fibrils. The cap underside is off-white, covered in short white tubes ending in pores. The whole mass can weigh several kilograms.
HABITAT At the base of oak trees, or rarely on other broadleaf trees. Autumn.
POSSIBLE CONFUSION *Polyporus umbellatus* has the same habitat but its caps are paler brown or grey and flatter.
EDIBILITY Edible only when young.

Giant Polypore
■ *Meripilus giganteus*
Diameter <2m, thickness 0.5–2cm

SYNONYM *Polyporus giganteus*.
DESCRIPTION This polypore forms massive, imbricated brackets that can weigh 12kg or more. The tough caps are welded laterally at the base in a deformed stump or pseudo-stem. The upper surface of the caps or brackets is covered in reddish-brown to sepia rings on a paler background. The flesh is white at first, turning darker and eventually blackening. The underside is white, darkening when cut or bruised, and eventually turning black from the spores. The tubes are white, ending in small pores.
HABITAT Completely covers Beech *Fagus sylvatica* or oak stumps. Summer and autumn.
EDIBILITY Edible but of little culinary interest.

Dyer's Mazegill

■ *Phaeolus schweinitzii*
Diameter 10–30cm

SYNONYM *Polyporus schweinitzii*.
DESCRIPTION The bracket is sulphur-yellow at first and irregular in shape. It then forms a circular or kidney-shaped cap that turns rust-brown with a yellow margin. The velvety upper surface of the bracket is irregular, cracked and pitted. The flesh is yellow and spongy, later turning brown. The tubes are wide and elongated, ending in pores on a yellowish-brown underside.
HABITAT On the branches or roots of dead or dying conifers. Summer and autumn.
EDIBILITY Not edible. As its common name implies, this fungus is used to make a dye in northern Europe, producing a range of colours from yellow to brown and green, depending on the type of mordant used.

Chicken of the Woods

■ *Laetiporus sulphureus*
Diameter 15–20cm

SYNONYMS Sulphur Polypore, *Polyporus sulphureus*.
DESCRIPTION This distinctive polypore has imbricated caps that are brilliant orange, with a wide yellow banded margin. The brackets are lobed and deformed, growing straight from the tree without a stem, superimposed and often in large tufts. The flesh is white, tending to yellow with age, soft and brittle. The underside is yellow. The flavour and smell of the raw fungus is pleasant, sometimes spicy.
HABITAT A dangerous parasite on deciduous and coniferous trees, continuing to live on them after it has killed them, although it can also be found growing on dead stumps. Spring to autumn.
EDIBILITY Edible when young; highly prized in the USA.

Root Rot

■ *Heterobasidion annosum*
Diameter 1–40cm

SYNONYMS *Fomes annosus,
Polyporus annosum, Ungulina annosa*.
DESCRIPTION The fruiting bodies
may take the form of incrustations or
brackets. The upper surface is reddish
brown, darkening to brown and
then blackish, with a white margin.
The underside is white, with small,
crowded tubes ending in pores. New
layers of tubes form annually. When
conditions are humid, the fungus
produces asexual spores, known as
conidiophores, which can live in the

soil for 10 months. This stage has a separate scientific name, *Spiniger meineckellus*.
HABITAT A dangerous parasite destroying pine trees. The spores infect tree stumps or may
enter the tree through a wound caused by an insect. The mycelium moves into the root,
destroying it. Summer to autumn.
EDIBILITY Not edible.

Birch Polypore

■ *Piptoporus betulinus*
Diameter 10–25cm, height 3–10cm

SYNONYMS Razorstrop Fungus,
Polyporus betulinus.
DESCRIPTION The fruiting body
is rounded at first, rapidly spreading
into a fan-shaped, kidney-shaped
or circular bracket. The cuticle is
greyish brown to brown, thin and dry,
and flakes and chips away in patches.
The margin is whitish with a raised
rim that partially covers the pores at
the edge of the white underside. The
crowded tubes end in small, round

pores. The stem, where it exists, is
very short and lateral. The flesh is flexible at first, becoming corky in the mature specimen.
HABITAT Parasitic on birch trees, causing white rot. Autumn.
EDIBILITY Not edible. The alternative common name refers to the fact that pieces of the
fungus were once used to sharpen cut-throat razors.

Conifer Mazegill

▪ *Gloeophyllum sepiarium*
Diameter 12cm, height 1cm

SYNONYMS Brown Rot Polypore, Rusty-gilled Polypore, *Lenzites sepiarius*.
DESCRIPTION The fruiting body forms dense, fan-shaped, kidney-shaped or circular brackets that are fawn or greyish brown. The margin is paler, ranging from cream-coloured to bright orange. The flesh is leathery and rust-brown. The underside is covered in densely packed, gill-like structures arranged in a maze-like pattern, hence the common name. The gills are yellowish white in colour.
HABITAT The fungus grows as large numbers of imbricated caps on cut wood, worked wood or the stumps of conifers, mainly spruce, its rhizomorphs eating into the heartwood and causing brown rot. The fruiting bodies can be seen throughout the year, but they produce spores only in late summer to autumn.
EDIBILITY Not edible.

Red-belted Polypore

▪ *Fomitopsis pinicola* Diameter 10–25cm, height 3–10cm

SYNONYM *Ungulina marginata*.
DESCRIPTION The fruiting body forms large brackets that are flattened or hoof-shaped. The upper surface of the bracket is blackish, tough and resinous, and will melt if a flame is applied to it. The margin is paler, though not always red – it can be yellow, orange, or white with an orange or red band. The underside is pale yellow and sometimes drips a whitish latex.
HABITAT Parasitic. Fruiting bodies persist throughout the year, but spore formation occurs only in the autumn.
POSSIBLE CONFUSION The Rosy Cork *F. rosea* is similar but the whole bracket is pinkish, including the darker part, and it is not resinous. It is parasitic on conifers at high altitude.
EDIBILITY Not edible.

Hoof Fungus ■ *Fomes fomentarius*
Diameter 10–50cm, height 3–10cm

SYNONYMS Tinder Bracket, *Polyporus fomentarius*.

DESCRIPTION The large brackets may be hoof-shaped or spatulate. The upper surface is banded with brown striations against a paler background, and it is grey or blackish where the fungus is attached to the tree. The margin is white, yellowing with age. The underside is felty and brownish white, browning when bruised.

HABITAT Fruiting bodies persist throughout the year, mainly on birches but also on Beech *Fagus sylvatica* and Sycamore *Acer pseudoplatanus*. Spores are produced only in autumn, when a new growth is added.

EDIBILITY Not edible. The alternative name for the species relates to the fact that pieces of the fungus were once used for striking friction matches; it is still useful as a firelighter owing to its slow-burning property.

Blushing Bracket
■ *Daedaleopsis confragosa*
Diameter 15cm, height 2cm

DESCRIPTION The fruiting body forms large brackets that are flattened or hoof-shaped. The upper surface of the brackets is banded with brown striations against a paler background, and with a thick grey or blackish area where the stemless fungus is attached to the tree. The margin is white, yellowing with age. The underside is brownish white; the species' common name comes from the fact that the flesh browns or reddens when bruised.

HABITAT Grows singly or in groups on broadleaf trees, mainly birch, Beech *Fagus sylvatica* and willow. Found throughout the year, but spores are released only in autumn, when the new growth of tubes adds to the thickness of the bracket.

EDIBILITY Not edible.

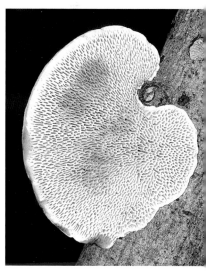

Oak Mazegill

▪ *Daedalea quercina*
Diameter 8–25cm, height 3–10cm

SYNONYM *Trametes quercina*.
DESCRIPTION The fruiting body forms large brackets that are kidney-shaped, semicircular or hoof-shaped, attached to the tree by a broad base. The upper surface of the brackets is banded with pale ochraceous-brown to darker brown striations, marked with concentric zones that are sometimes wrinkled, and edged with a whitish to pale ochre margin. The felty surface is pitted and tends to flake away in parts as the fungus ages. The extended, swollen white underside is covered in thick, forked, plate-like gills and also has elongated, irregular pores. The spores are white.
HABITAT On oak stumps or fallen branches; occasionally on Sweet Chestnut *Castanea sativa* or Horse-chestnut *Aesculus hippocastanum*. Year-round.
POSSIBLE CONFUSION Lumpy Bracket (p. 123).
EDIBILITY Not edible.

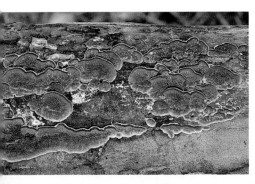

Purplepore Bracket

▪ *Trichaptum abietinum*
Diameter 0.5–3cm

SYNONYM *Coriolus abietinus*.
DESCRIPTION At first, the fruiting body covers the tree on which it grows like a crust, but eventually it forms kidney-shaped, semicircular or hoof-shaped brackets, which are attached directly without a stem. The irregular felty upper surface of the bracket is banded with greyish or brownish concentric rings, which in damp places may be greenish owing to the growth of algae. The underside is violet, with irregular pores that tear into coarse, pointed excrescences.
HABITAT Grows in huge numbers, sometimes hundreds of specimens, on the dead wood of conifers. Year-round.
POSSIBLE CONFUSION The Silverleaf Fungus (p. 140) is similar, but is paler in colour and grows on broadleaf trees.
EDIBILITY Not edible.

Lumpy Bracket
■ *Trametes gibbosa* Diameter 7–20cm

DESCRIPTION The fruiting body is a semicircular or scallop-shaped bracket attached directly to the tree. Both the upper surface and underside are white at first, although the upper surface may turn green where algae grow on it, especially in damp places. The upper surface is pitted and lumpy, with raised white bands at the margin. The flesh is white, and the pores are wide and elongated.

HABITAT Parasitic on broadleaf trees, especially Beech *Fagus sylvatica*; very occasionally found on conifers. Year-round.

POSSIBLE CONFUSION The Oak Mazegill (p. 122) is similar but has elongated and maze-like pores, and a coloured upper surface.

EDIBILITY Not edible.

Turkeytail
■ *Trametes versicolor* Diameter 5–20cm

SYNONYM *Coriolus versicolor*.
DESCRIPTION The fruiting body consists of concentric, circular or kidney-shaped brackets attached directly to the tree. The silky or velvety upper surface is covered in bands of various colours, shaded at the attached end from black to grey and brown, and with a white, cream or pale brown margin. The light brown flesh is flexible and leathery. The underside is whitish or cream, and is densely covered in pores.

HABITAT On dead stumps and branches of all types of broadleaf trees. Year-round.
POSSIBLE CONFUSION The Bleeding Oak Crust (p. 107) has a similar colouring, but unlike that species the Turkeytail does not exude blood-red droplets.
EDIBILITY Not edible.

Smoky Bracket ▪ *Bjerkandera adusta*
Diameter 5–8cm

SYNONYMS Burnt Polypore, *Leptoporus adustus*.
DESCRIPTION This small greyish-white fungus grows in dense, imbricated brackets. The brackets are shallow and fan-shaped at first, later becoming kidney-shaped, and have an undulating white margin. The surface is downy when young, then smooth. The whitish flesh is flexible but leathery. The greyish tubes are short and the pores are small. The underside is cinder-grey, sometimes blackish, giving the fungus the appearance of having been blackened by smoke – hence its common name.
HABITAT On dead wood, especially Beech *Fagus sylvatica*, and occasionally on other broadleaf trees. Often in large groups of several hundred specimens. Spring to autumn.
POSSIBLE CONFUSION Big Smoky Bracket *B. fumosa* is similar but is thicker, has a white underside and smells of aniseed.
EDIBILITY Not edible.

Artist's Bracket
▪ *Ganoderma applanatum*
Diameter <70cm

SYNONYM *G. lipsiense*.
DESCRIPTION Can grow to an enormous size, and consists of a scallop-shaped or irregular bracket with a very uneven upper surface covered in concentric furrows. It is whitish, then brownish black, often with a dusting of chocolate-brown spores. The tubes are brown, and grow a new layer every year. The leathery flesh can be 10–15cm thick. The underside is white in young specimens. The fungus is sometimes covered in black galls produced by the fly *Agathomya wankowiczi*.
HABITAT Grows on dead branches of deciduous trees, rarely on conifers. Year-round.
EDIBILITY Not edible. So called because the underside can be used for drawing pictures, as it turns brown where pressure is applied.

Ganoderma resinaceum
Diameter <30cm

DESCRIPTION The irregularly shaped bracket is dark reddish brown in colour, with a thick yellow band of resin at the margin. The band is irregular, sometimes very wide, almost covering the whole bracket, and soon hardens. The resin can be melted by holding a lighter flame to it. The flesh is tough and 6–10cm thick. The underside is white with yellowish tubes, releasing chocolate-coloured spores that stain the surrounding tree bark.
HABITAT Parasitic on various species of oak. The fungus has a 2-year cycle, the bracket decaying and dying at the end of this period and being replaced by fresh brackets growing above, below or around it. Year-round.
EDIBILITY Not edible.

Sessile Earthstar
■ *Geastrum fimbriatum*
Fruiting body diameter 2–5cm

SYNONYMS G. *sessile.*
DESCRIPTION The earthstars comprise a circular sac containing the spores (the endoperidium), surrounded by a protective covering that splits open into a star shape (the exoperidium). In the Sessile Earthstar, the endoperidium is about 2.5cm in diameter and looks like a miniature, slightly deflated whitish football. The brown spores emerge from a hole in the top. The stalk is absent or very short. The rays of the star-shaped exoperidium are a slightly darker brown; they bend back under the endoperidium when the fungus is mature and crack in dry weather.
HABITAT Found under broadleaf and coniferous trees; prefers clay soil. Summer and autumn.
EDIBILITY Not edible.

Collared Earthstar

■ *Geastrum triplex*
Fruiting body diameter 4–15cm

DESCRIPTION Has the common name Collared Earthstar because it has an extra, third, fleshy layer between the endoperidium, which contains the spores, and the exoperidium, which bursts open into a star shape. The immature fungus is the shape of a tulip bulb. The endoperidium, when exposed, is pale grey-brown, while the rest of the flesh is slightly pinkish white. The additional layer of flesh often cracks in dry weather, peeling away to form a cup around the endoperidium. The black spores are dispersed in puffs when a raindrop or other missile hits the endoperidium, or are wafted away by wind.
HABITAT Prefers warm, shady places in thick woods, especially under broadleaf trees. Jul–Oct.
EDIBILITY Not edible.

Striate Earthstar ■ *Geastrum striatum*

Fruiting body diameter 4–15cm

SYNONYM G. *bryantii*.
DESCRIPTION The ball-shaped endoperidium is at first enclosed inside a cup formed by the 6–12 fleshy reddish-brown rays of the exoperidium. As the fungus matures, the rays turn back on themselves so that their tips point towards the ground, completely exposing the pale or dark grey endoperidium, which is raised above the rays on a short stalk. The endoperidium has a distinct collar at the base and a beak-like, striated ostiole, from which the dark brown spores emerge. The fruiting body is paler in dry weather.
HABITAT On the ground in deciduous woods and on heaths and dunes. Probably not native to Europe. Autumn.
EDIBILITY Not edible.

Arched Earthstar

■ *Geastrum fornicatum*
Fruiting body diameter 5–10cm

DESCRIPTION As in the Striate Earthstar
(p. 126), the endoperidium is exposed only
when the spores are mature. The 4 rays of the
exoperidium at first cover the endoperidium
completely, but peel back and split into 2 layers
to expose it. The endoperidium is ball-shaped,
velvety and dark brown, and is borne on a
short stalk. The tips of the reddish-brown rays
stay attached to the whitish outer layer of the
exoperidium, whose cup-shaped remains raise
the fungus off the ground. The dark brown spores
emerge through a ragged pore. The species was
first described in 1688 by G. Seger, who named it
Fungus anthropomorphus since he thought it looked
like a manikin.
HABITAT Associated with deciduous trees in
groups. Apr–Nov.
EDIBILITY Not edible.

Fluted Bird's Nest

■ *Cyathus striatus* Diameter
0.5–1cm, height 1–1.5cm

DESCRIPTION The bird's
nest fungi are so tiny they can
easily be overlooked by fungus-
hunters. In the Fluted Bird's
Nest, the 10–15 'eggs' (known
as peridioles) that enclose the
spores are at first covered with a
white membrane, this splitting
open when the peridioles are
ripe. The peridioles are ovoid,
pale grey at first and turning
brown when mature. The 'nest',
or exoperidium, is dark brown
on the outside and covered with stiff, tangled brown hairs; it is fluted and greyish on the
inside. The fungus relies on raindrops to detach the peridioles and disperse them.
HABITAT On rotting and mossy twigs or branches. Summer to autumn.
EDIBILITY Not edible.

Common Bird's Nest

▪ *Crucibulum laeve*
Diameter 8mm, height 1–1.5cm

SYNONYM Orange Bird's Nest.
DESCRIPTION The peridioles are at the bottom of a bucket-shaped 'nest' that at first is covered by a hairy orange membrane. This then opens to disclose a white membrane, which subsequently tears to reveal the dozen or so disc-shaped peridioles that are pale ochre at first and turn white when ripe. The peridioles are attached to the nest by a string known as a funiculus; this breaks under pressure, one end remaining attached to the peridiole. The loose end is adhesive, allowing the peridiole to attach itself to any host with which it comes into contact.
HABITAT On the ground on leaf litter, humus and rotting wood. Spring to autumn.
EDIBILITY Not edible.

Pestle Puffball

▪ *Lycoperdon excipuliforme*
Diameter <12cm, height 10–20cm

SYNONYMS *Calvatia excipuliformis*, *Handkea excipuliformis*.
DESCRIPTION Although this fungus is a member of the puffballs, it is shaped like a thick white pestle. The bulbous top is of a piece with the tall, cylindrical pseudo-stem, which is often yellowish at the base. The exoperidium, the covering on the top that hides the spore mass, is granulose or covered in tiny spines or excrescences.
HABITAT On the ground under broadleaf trees and conifers, sometimes in grass where no trees are evident, and usually on clay soil. Summer and autumn.
EDIBILITY Edible only when the flesh is white, in the young stage, but the exoperidium should be discarded.

Dusky Puffball

■ *Lycoperdon nigrescens*
Diameter 2–3.5cm, height 2–5cm

SYNONYMS *L. foetidum, L. perlatum* var. *nigrescens*.
DESCRIPTION The dark fruiting body is globe- or pear-shaped, with or without a pseudo-stem. The papery exoperidium is tan or buff, covered in tiny brown or blackish spines that are often joined at the tip and leave a reticulate pattern on the endoperidium when shed. A pore opens at the top at maturity to release the olive-coloured spores. The gleba is white at first, darkening at maturity.
HABITAT Solitary or in small groups in pinewoods and, occasionally, broadleaf woods. Autumn to early winter.
POSSIBLE CONFUSION The similar Umber Puffball *L. umbrinum* is blackish brown with no reddish tinge, and has spines and warts that leave no trace when shed. It is edible when young.
EDIBILITY Not edible.

Common Puffball

■ *Lycoperdon perlatum*
Head diameter 3–5cm, height 5–12cm

SYNONYM *L. gemmatum*.
DESCRIPTION This all-white Puffball is pestle-shaped, with a bulbous head on a pseudo-stem that is rounded and narrows at the base. The head is covered in tiny, irregular granules, blunt spines or warts that can easily be rubbed off, leaving rounded pits. The flesh is spongy. The gleba is white when young, turning yellowish, then olive and powdery when the spores mature. It is at this stage that a ragged pore opens in the top and the spores drift out on the wind.
HABITAT In mixed woods and meadows. Summer and autumn.
EDIBILITY Edible only when the gleba is white. Used in folk medicine in France as a styptic and to aid digestion.

Stump Puffball

■ *Lycoperdon pyriforme* Diameter 2–5cm

SYNONYM *L. saccatum*.

DESCRIPTION A pear-shaped puffball with a thin exoperidium on a pseudo-stem that narrows at the base. It is white at first and covered in warty spines, turning pale brown as the gleba inside matures and then losing spines. The gleba is soft and spongy; it is white when young, turning yellowish, and then olive and powdery when the spores mature and emerge from a hole at the top.

HABITAT On rotting wood. Often grows in large numbers of tightly packed specimens. Summer to early winter.

POSSIBLE CONFUSION Similar to Common and Scaly earthballs (p. 132), but with thinner exoperidium and they are suspect or, in the case of Scaly Earthball, slightly poisonous.

EDIBILITY Edible only when the gleba is white.

Giant Puffball

■ *Calvatia gigantea*
Diameter 30cm or more

SYNONYM *Langermannia gigantea*.

DESCRIPTION This unmistakable mushroom is almost certainly the largest of the macrofungi and may weigh several kilograms (a specimen found in Hungary weighed 20 kg). It appears to be lying on its side, and from one angle looks like the top of a human skull. The exoperidium is white or yellowish, easily separable from the gleba inside,

and tears open when mature. The gleba is white when young, turning yellowish, and then olive-coloured and powdery when the spores mature and emerge from a hole at the top.

HABITAT In well-manured grassland and parks, in shady spots. Summer to early winter.

EDIBILITY Edible only when the gleba is white.

Meadow Puffball

■ *Vascellum pratense*
Diameter 2–5cm

SYNONYM *Lycoperdon pratense*.
DESCRIPTION Has a slightly
flattened top and pointed base,
forming a short, thick pseudo-stem
whose flesh is spongy. It is white at
first and covered with tiny spines that
disappear with age. The exoperidium
turns pale brown as the gleba inside
matures. When cut open, the gleba is
revealed to inhabit only the top of the
fungus. When the olive spores mature,
they emerge from a hole at the top.
HABITAT On grass verges and in
meadows. Summer and autumn.
POSSIBLE CONFUSION Similar to
the Common and Scaly earthballs
(p. 132), but those species have a thick exoperidium.
EDIBILITY Edible only when the gleba is white.

Grey Puffball

■ *Bovista plumbea* Diameter 1–3.5cm

SYNONYM Leaden Puffball.
DESCRIPTION Completely round
with a thin exoperidium that is
white in the immature specimen.
It gradually tears or flakes away to
reveal a leaden-grey endoperidium
that contains the gleba. The spores
are olive-green, emerging when ripe
through a small hole that tears in the
top of the fungus.
HABITAT On well-manured grass
verges and in meadows. Unlike
other puffballs, the Grey Puffball
is not securely anchored to the soil
and the papery endoperidium often
blows away in the wind. Summer and
autumn.
EDIBILITY Not edible.

Common Earthball

■ *Scleroderma citrinum*
Diameter 4–12cm, height 4–8cm

DESCRIPTION Looks like a flattened sphere, cream-coloured or beige, occasionally orange, covered in coarse, angular brownish warts. The exoperidium is thicker than that of a puffball, but as in a puffball it tears open at the top so that the black spores of the gleba can escape. The base rests on cottony white mycelial cords that attach it to the soil. The gleba is white at first, then pink and eventually violet-black, marbled with white veins.

HABITAT Often grows in groups, on siliceous soil among trees and in grassland. It is sometimes parasitised by the Parasitic Bolete (p. 23). Summer and autumn.

POSSIBLE CONFUSION The Stump and Meadow puffballs (pp. 130 and 131) are similar, but in those species the exoperidium is thinner.

EDIBILITY Not edible; suspect.

Scaly Earthball

■ *Scleroderma verrucosum*
Diameter 3–8cm, height 6–10cm

DESCRIPTION Looks like an irregular brownish-ochre or reddish sphere that is fragmented into small, irregular scales or blunt spines, mainly around the top, although despite its common name it is much less scaly than the Common Earthball (*above*). It sits on a thick, short, pitted pseudo-stem, ending in mycelial filaments, which raises it off the ground. The gleba inside is white at first, eventually darkening as the dark brown spores mature.

HABITAT In parks and gardens near trees, especially oaks, in warm places rich in humus and on sandy soil. Summer and autumn.

POSSIBLE CONFUSION *S. cepa* is similar but the spines are less prominent and the pseudo-stem, if present, is much shorter. The Stump and Meadow puffballs (pp. 130 and 131) are also similar, but in those species the exoperidium is thinner.

EDIBILITY **Slightly poisonous**.

Winter Stalkball

■ *Tulostoma brumale*
Diameter 1cm, height 2–3cm

SYNONYM *T. mammosum*.
DESCRIPTION This odd-looking fungus
is as unusual as its habitat. It consists of a
tall brownish or greyish stem, darkening
at the base, which may be smooth or scaly,
and which is often completely buried in the
substrate. The base is bulbous and covered
with a volva in which debris accumulates.
The stem is topped with a little greyish or
whitish sub-spherical or flattened head that
is darker where it joins the stem. There is
a clearly defined ostiole in the top, from
which the spores emerge.
HABITAT In arid places, such as dunes,
chalky grassland and garden rockeries,
where it is often mistaken for rabbit
droppings. Summer and autumn.
EDIBILITY Not edible.

Earpick Fungus

■ *Auriscalpium vulgare*
Cap 1–2cm, height 5–9cm

DESCRIPTION Consists of a tiny, almost
circular, pale brown cap that is covered
in brown hairs, and whose underside is
covered in tiny spines that do not extend
to the margin. The long, slender stem is
pale brown, darkening to black at the base,
and is covered in stiff dark brown hairs. It
is attached to the cap laterally. The spines,
which are covered with the spore-bearing
hymenium, are greyish white, darkening
when the spores are mature and white.
HABITAT On pinecones, sometimes buried
in moss. Summer and autumn.
EDIBILITY Not edible. The species'
common name is an allusion to the
implement used by the Romans to clean
their ears.

Coral Tooth

■ *Hericium coralloides*
Diameter 8–50cm

SYNONYMS *H. flagellum*,
H. ramosum, *Dryodon coralloides*.
DESCRIPTION This large cream
or white fungus looks like a type of
stalagmitic rock formation or coral,
hanging in a huge mass of ramified
branches originating from a single
stem. It bears brittle spines about
1–2cm in length, which are often
grouped or welded together and hang
in rows along the delicate branches of
the fungus. The flesh and spores are
white.
HABITAT Saprophitic on the fallen
branches and logs of broadleaf trees. Possibly parasitic, entering the wood through a wound
caused by damage or an insect. Late summer and autumn.
POSSIBLE CONFUSION The related Wavy Coral Tooth *Creolophus cirrhatus* is similar but
branches into spiny, imbricated caps.
EDIBILITY Edible only when young.

Bearded Tooth

■ *Hericium erinaceus*
Diameter 10–25cm

SYNONYMS Lion's Mane Mushroom,
Monkey Head Mushroom, *Dryodon
erinaceum*, *Hydnum erinaceum*.
DESCRIPTION The massive cream
or white cap or head is virtually
spherical, growing from a sturdy,
short stem. Tightly packed spines as
long as 4cm cover the entire head,
hanging from the front and underside.
These spines are covered with the
spore-bearing hymenium. The flesh
is gelatinous when young, leathery when old, and the spores are white.
HABITAT On the fallen branches of broadleaf trees. Autumn until the 1st frosts.
EDIBILITY Edible when young. It is cultivated on sawdust by the Chinese, Japanese and
Koreans. It is also a traditional Chinese medicinal remedy, and modern science has shown
it to have antioxidant and hypoglycaemic properties.

Beefsteak Fungus

■ *Fistulina hepatica*
Width 6–25cm, thickness 2–6cm

DESCRIPTION Starting from a
shapeless red lump growing on the
side of a tree, the Beefsteak Fungus
expands into a bright red bracket
or tongue-shaped fungus. The size,
shape and consistency are those of an
ox-tongue. The slimy cuticle is easily
separable from the flesh and is covered
in small papillae like a tongue, and
the crimson colour is similar to that
of fresh ox or calf's liver. The tubes
containing the spores are yellow at
first and then red, and are attached to each other but separable. The underside is yellowish
and then pinkish red, with small, round pores. The stem is short or absent.
HABITAT Parasitic on oak, Sweet Chestnut *Castanea sativa* and Horse-chestnut *Aesculus
hippocastanum*, in which it causes brown rot. Summer and autumn.
EDIBILITY Edible when young, even raw.

Willow Bracket

■ *Phellinus igniarius*
Diameter 15–20cm, thickness 5–15cm

SYNONYM *Ochroporus ignarius*.
DESCRIPTION This polypore is clog-
or hoof-shaped, with an upper surface
covered in pits, nodules and ridges.
The colour varies from cinnamon-
brown in young specimens to greyish
black as it matures. The underside is
reddish brown, darkening to grey, and
is covered in small pores. The flesh is
brown and has a woody consistency.
HABITAT Parasitic on the trunks of
willow, Ash *Fraxinus excelsior* and fruit
trees, causing brown rot. Year-round,
but the pores grow a new layer in the
autumn.
EDIBILITY Not edible. This fungus was burned and the ash mixed with tobacco by Native
American peoples, since the alkaloid it contains enhances the pleasurable effect of
smoking.

Alder Bracket ▪ *Inonotus radiatus*
Diameter 2–9cm, thickness 1–2cm

SYNONYMS Brown Cushion Polypore, Cinnamon Polypore.

DESCRIPTION The upper surface of this polypore is covered in ridges; older specimens are faintly banded in different shades of brown towards the margin. The colour is apricot at first, darkening to rust-brown and finally blackish. The thin, well-defined margin is pale yellow. The flesh is rust-coloured and woody, with a faintly sweetish smell. The tubes are rust-brown. The underside is brown and covered in circular or angular pores. The stem is lateral or absent. The spores are ochraceous to pale brown.

HABITAT Parasitic on alders and certain other deciduous trees, including fruit trees. Year-round, with new growth in the autumn.

EDIBILITY Not edible.

Cinder Conk ▪ *Inonotus obliquus*
Diameter <1.5m, thickness 40cm

SYNONYMS Chaga, Clinker Polypore, White Birch Tinder Fungus.

DESCRIPTION There are 2 stages to the life cycle of this fungus: the first imperfect, asexual stage (illustrated) forms an ugly black mass, parasitic on living tree trunks. It is dense, hard, cracked and brittle on the surface, appearing to have been burnt. The corky flesh is yellow-brown, containing white strands. The underside is dark brown. The second perfect stage produces spores from inconspicuous patches in the cracks of the imperfect stage or neighbouring bark.

HABITAT Parasitic on alder, birch, Beech *Fagus sylvatica* and other deciduous trees. Year-round, with new growth in the autumn.

EDIBILITY Edible. Recent experiments have shown that its active principles shrink cancer tumours and combat a range of infections.

Oak Curtain Crust

■ *Hymenochaete rubiginosa*
Diameter 5–25cm, thickness 1–4cm

SYNONYM *Stereum rubiginosa*.
DESCRIPTION Attached at the top of the bracket to the tree, the bottom hanging away in the shape of a ruched or wavy curtain, hence the species' common name. The top is velvety, shaded in bands from purplish blue, where it is attached, to paler rust colour, and there is a clearly defined yellow margin. The smooth, spore-bearing hymenium on the underside is rust-brown.
HABITAT On logs and cut wood of broadleaf trees, especially oak and Sweet Chestnut *Castanea sativa*. Year-round.
POSSIBLE CONFUSION The Tobacco Curtain Crust *H. tabacina* looks similar, but its bands are rust-red and it prefers willows and Hazel *Corylus avellana*.
EDIBILITY Not edible.

Tiger's Eye ■ *Coltricia perennis*
Cap <8cm, height 2–5cm

DESCRIPTION This unusual polypore has been mistakenly classified as a bolete (pp. 16–23) in the past. The funnel-shaped, velvety cap is covered in rings coloured from cinnamon to orange on a yellow background. The white underside is covered in tiny pores, the ends of the cinnamon-brown tubes. The brown flesh is corky. The spores are yellow-brown.
HABITAT On sandy, acid soils in woods and on heaths. Autumn to early winter.
POSSIBLE CONFUSION The Woolly Velvet Polypore *Onnia tomentosa* looks similar, but the cap is plain brown with a velvety texture, the flesh is thicker and it grows only on dead conifers.
EDIBILITY Not edible.

Zoned Rosette

■ *Podoscypha multizonata*
Head 10–30cm, height 10–20cm

SYNONYMS *Phlacteria multizonata, Stereum multizonatum, Thelephora multizonata*.
DESCRIPTION This branching fungus looks like a frisée or butter lettuce, its branches flattened like leaves that are folded or grow in circles in a rosette formation on a short rooting stem. The edges of the branches are thin, lobed and brownish, with darker areas. The colour of the underside is violet-grey to violet-orange.
HABITAT Under oaks and other broadleaf trees, sometimes on buried wood, possibly growing on the roots. Autumn.
POSSIBLE CONFUSION May be mistaken for species of *Thelephora* polypores, such as the very variable Earthfan (p. 142), but that species generally grows on rotting conifer logs and pine cones, including buried wood. May also be confused with the Wood Cauliflower (p. 113).
EDIBILITY Not edible.

Yellow Brain ■ *Tremella mesenterica*
Diameter 2–8cm

DESCRIPTION This slightly translucent, brightly coloured, lemon-yellow or orange-yellow jelly fungus starts as a small lump and builds up into a convoluted, folded, lobed mass. It flattens in dry weather and becomes tough and leathery, which prevents it from drying out, but then swells again in wet weather. Some examples are not so brightly coloured and may be olive-green or even white. The spores are white.
HABITAT On the branches of various broadleaf trees. Spring to autumn.
POSSIBLE CONFUSION May be mistaken for other brightly coloured jelly fungi such as the Leafy Brain *T. foliacea*, which is reddish brown but has the same indeterminate shape, as well as with Beech Jellydisc (p. 147) and species of *Dacrymyces* or *Ditiola*, all of which are also jelly fungi.
EDIBILITY Edible.

Jew's Ear ■ *Auricularia auricula-judae*

Diameter 4–10cm

SYNONYMS Jelly Ear, *Hirneola auricula-judae*.

DESCRIPTION This jelly fungus is indeed ear-shaped, being thin, lobed and veined, and has a very short or absent stem. The outer surface (generally the upper surface) may be reddish brown, greyish or even greenish. The velvety appearance is accentuated with age. The inner, spore-bearing surface is shiny. The thin flesh is translucent.

HABITAT On fallen deciduous tree trunks of many species, but especially Elder *Sambucus nigra*. The common name is a shortened version of 'Judas's Ear', a reference to the fact that after betraying Jesus, Judas is said to have hanged himself on an Elder tree. Year-round.

EDIBILITY Edible and delicious. A related species, Cloud Ear *A. polytricha*, is popular in Southeast Asia as a food and a medicine.

Tripe Fungus

■ *Auricularia mesenterica*

Diameter 5–15cm, thickness 0.3–0.5cm

DESCRIPTION This jelly fungus is off-white with greyish or brownish areas on the upper side. The zoning or ribbing on the top is the result of growth lines, as the fungus produces a new hymenium (fertile layer) every year. The greyish-violet hymenium is on the underside, and has folded or ribbed areas, a little like tripe. The edges are lobed and veined, and the stem is very short or absent. The flesh is tough and leathery.

HABITAT On dying or dead deciduous trees, especially Ash *Fraxinus excelsior*, causing a white rot. Year-round, but grows mainly in spring and autumn.

EDIBILITY Edible but of little interest. Used for medicinal purposes in parts of eastern Europe.

Silverleaf Fungus

■ *Chondrostereum purpureum*
Diameter 1–3cm

DESCRIPTION This fungus starts life as a crust on wood. The fruiting body then develops into a series of ruffled purple brackets growing along the branches and trunks of trees. The upper surface is pale brown with concentric rings and a pale margin, which is sometimes greyish; it is covered in off-white hairs. When the fruiting bodies dry out, they turn brown.

HABITAT Grows on the cut branches of broadleaf trees, breaking down the wood. A dangerous pest on fruit trees, especially plums, causing silverleaf disease. Year-round, adding a new layer of growth annually between spring and autumn.

POSSIBLE CONFUSION Purplepore Bracket (p. 122) is similar, but is darker and grows on conifers.

EDIBILITY Not edible.

Wrinkled Crust

■ *Phlebia radiata* Diameter <15cm

SYNONYMS *P. aurantiaca*, *P. radiata*.

DESCRIPTION This mass of shapeless yellowish fungus varies in colour from pale yellow to deep orange, though dried-up specimens are greyish and hard. It covers the host in a series of lobed, folded and pleated, radiating patches or crusts, for which the technical term is resupinate. The irregular surface may also be violet. The margin is torn, in various shades of orange. The reason for the species' common name is that the centre of each patch is covered in wrinkles.

HABITAT On the mossy bark of broadleaf trees. Year-round, but grows only in spring and summer.

POSSIBLE CONFUSION Similar to *P. rufa*, but that species is not folded on itself and is covered in pores.

EDIBILITY Not edible.

Jelly Rot

■ *Phlebia tremellosa*
Diameter 5–15cm

SYNONYMS Trembling Rot, *Merulius tremellosus*.
DESCRIPTION The distorted caps of the Jelly Rot are white to pale yellow, hairy and woolly. It forms gelatinous crusts or slightly raised brackets on the branches on which it grows, the caps overlapping and growing together. The underside, the fertile hymenium, is covered in a network of radiating folds, ridges, veins and anastomosed pores, from which the spores emerge. It is yellow or pale brown, darkening to orange and then brown as the spores mature. The thin flesh has a rubbery or gelatinous texture.
HABITAT On the fallen branches or stumps of deciduous trees, more rarely on conifers. Summer and autumn.
EDIBILITY Not edible.

Scaly Tooth

■ *Sarcodon squamosus*
Diameter 10–20cm,
height 6–13cm

SYNONYM Turtle Mushroom.
DESCRIPTION The hedgehog mushrooms are so called because they disperse their spores from the underside of the cap on spines. The cap of the Scaly Tooth is ochraceous-brown or reddish, covered in blackish-brown scales outlined in white, resembling the back of a turtle. The flesh is white and mild. The short white stem darkens and narrows towards the base. The short (5–10mm) spines are slightly decurrent and greyish blue when young, darkening to greyish.
HABITAT Under pine trees. Autumn.
POSSIBLE CONFUSION Resembles the Scaly Hedgehog *S. imbricatus*, which has brown scales and grows at altitude.
EDIBILITY Edible, although opinions vary as to quality. Also used as a dye.

Woolly Tooth

■ *Phellodon tomentosus*
Diameter 2–5cm, height 3–7cm

SYNONYMS Tough Hedgehog, *Calodon tomentosus*, *Hydnum sciathiforme*.
DESCRIPTION The funnel-shaped cap has a fluffy, velvety texture and a scalloped or uneven edge. It is ringed with concentric bands of reddish brown in varying shades, with a white margin; the caps often become filled with plant debris as the fungus ages. The spines are short, decurrent and grey. The stem is very short and reddish brown. The very tough, leathery flesh is whitish and has a spicy smell, described as being like that of curry. The spores are white.

HABITAT On acid soil in pine forests at altitude. Like other members of the genus, it grows in large numbers, several caps being welded together. Autumn.
EDIBILITY Not edible.

Earthfan ■ *Thelephora terrestris*
Diameter 5–15cm, height 2–3cm

DESCRIPTION This fungus is very variable in appearance. It has an irregular surface of radiating, fan-shaped or frilly caps, sometimes growing in a rosette formation. The cap is covered in hairs, ringed concentrically in various shades of brown, and has a wide white margin that extends right underneath. The rest of the blackish underside is wrinkled and warty, cinnamon-brown and covered in pores. The brown flesh is tough and fibrous. The short stem, if present, is blackish. The spores are purple-brown.

HABITAT On pine-needle litter, occasionally under broadleaf trees. Grows in large groups that are imbricated or welded together, often covering a large area. Summer and autumn.
POSSIBLE CONFUSION Zoned Rosette (p. 138).
EDIBILITY Not edible.

Wood Hedgehog

■ *Hydnum repandum*
Cap 5–10cm, height 5–10cm

DESCRIPTION The fleshy cap of
this typical hedgehog fungus is very
irregular in shape. The velvety
cream-coloured cap is often pitted
and lumpy. The pale beige cuticle
is dry and smooth. The thick but
fragile margin is deeply inrolled,
becoming lobed and sinuous. The
flesh is thick and white. The spines
on the underside are brittle and
white, then cream. The spores are
white. The stem is thick, short and
white, often shorter than the diameter of the cap.
HABITAT Grows in large numbers, sometimes in circles, under conifers and broadleaf trees
at low altitude. Autumn and well into winter (it can withstand temperatures as low as
–5°C).
EDIBILITY Edible, especially when young.

Ergot ■ *Claviceps purpurea*
Diameter 1–2mm, length 5–6cm

DESCRIPTION Ergot emerges from a
root-like mass of mycelium (known
as a sclerotium) that appears between
the grains of ears of Rye *Secale cereale*.
The fruiting body is divided into a
thin, curving pseudo-stem covered in
felty white mycelium at the base, and a
small, round orange head that is pierced
with pores, from which the black spores
emerge.
HABITAT Mainly parasitic on Rye. Also
visible in the form of a sclerotium that
has fallen on the ground and survived
from the previous season. Year-round but
produces spores only in summer.
EDIBILITY Poisonous. The cause of a
range of symptoms known as St Anthony's
fire, but also valued as medicine owing to
its vasoconstrictive properties.

Snaketongue Truffleclub

■ *Cordyceps ophioglossoides*
Diameter 1cm, length 28cm

SYNONYM Truffleclub.
DESCRIPTION The long, snake-like reddish-brown or black fruiting body is devoid of a cap, but is divided into an upper part on which the spore-bearing hymenium is borne; it is dark and has a yellowish to black pseudo-stem. The flesh is black, as are the spores. The thick yellow mycelial cords at the base are rhizomorphs that connect this fungus parasite to its host.
HABITAT Like all species of *Cordyceps*, this fungus is parasitic, in this case on the False Truffle (p. 145). Late summer and autumn.
POSSIBLE CONFUSION May be mistaken for a dark club fungus such as the Earthtongue *Geoglossum nigritum*, which has a similar habitat but is not parasitic.
EDIBILITY Not edible.

Scarlet Caterpillarclub

■ *Cordyceps militaris* Height 5–6cm

DESCRIPTION The scientific name of this distinctive red parasite derives from its colour, which is reminiscent of the red of a British soldier's dress uniform. The club is often sinuous and thickened, with what appears to be a rough surface, but which actually consists of ostioles through which the white spores emerge. A white asexual stage of the fungus precedes the sexual stage, and has the separate scientific name of *Isaria farinosa*.
HABITAT Parasitic on larvae, nymphs and butterfly caterpillars, especially those that live on pine trees. The mycelium of the fungus totally invades the insect's body.
EDIBILITY Not edible and not to be handled without gloves, as both the parasite and its host are skin irritants.

False Truffle ■ *Elaphomyces granulatus*
Diameter 2–4cm

SYNONYM *E. cervinus*.
DESCRIPTION Rounded or oval like a
truffle. The surface is grey-brown or reddish
brown and covered in tiny warts. The wall
of the outer covering is relatively thick
and consists of 3 layers, yellow, white
and reddish brown. The gleba inside
is blackish brown, marbled with red.
HABITAT Found in association with
conifers or broadleaf trees. It is hypogeous,
spending its entire life cycle underground,
and is parasitised by the Snaketongue Truffleclub
(p. 144). Year-round.
POSSIBLE CONFUSION *E. muricatus* looks similar, but its shape is more pointed,
the inside is whitish, and it has an unpleasant odour; it is also parasitised by the
Snaketongue Truffleclub.
EDIBILITY Not edible.

Hairy Earthtongue
■ *Trichoglossum hirsutum* Height 7.5cm

SYNONYMS Velvety Black Earthtongue,
Velvety Earthtongue.
DESCRIPTION This small, dark fungus
is shiny yet velvety to the touch, as it is
covered in short, dark hairs. Despite being
club- or spade-shaped, it is not a fairy club,
but is in fact an ascomycete related to the
Bog Beacon (p. 146). The whole fungus,
both head and pseudo-stem, are covered in
velvety spines known as setae, which give
it both its common and scientific names;
these are visible through a hand lens.
HABITAT On decayed wood, in bogs and
on *Sphagnum* moss. Autumn.
POSSIBLE CONFUSION Experts claim
that the name actually covers up to
6 species, but these are separable only
by their microscopic characteristics.
Some lack the setae.
EDIBILITY Not edible.

Bog Beacon

■ *Mitrula paludosa* Height 4–6cm

DESCRIPTION This small, club-shaped ascomycete is easy to spot owing to its startling colour, growing as it does in drab surroundings. It looks like a red or orange beacon or a lighted match, since the top is brightly coloured and the pseudo-stem is yellow or off-white. Its irregular, rounded top contains the spore-bearing hymenium. The stem is hollow. HABITAT As its common name implies, the Bog Beacon is found growing in large numbers in *Sphagnum* moss in bogs and sodden moorland, as well as in ditches and depressions. Sometimes found on submerged vegetation. Spring to autumn. EDIBILITY Not edible.

Jellybaby ■ *Leotia lubrica*
Diameter 0.5–2cm, height 1–5cm

DESCRIPTION This jelly fungus is roughly the shape of a classic mushroom, since it has a small cap growing on a long stem. The convex cap is irregular, rounded or lobed, and wrinkled; it is olive or ochre in colour. The curving, winding stem is paler, being whitish to yellowish. Both cap and stem have a slimy coating. The stem is either gelatinous or hollow. HABITAT Grows in large clusters, often from the same point, on bare ground or among moss under conifers, more rarely in Beech woods. Sometimes found growing on well-rotted wood. Summer and autumn. POSSIBLE CONFUSION Chicken Lips *L. viscosa* looks similar but the cap is green. EDIBILITY Not edible.

Black Bulgar ▪ *Bulgaria inquinans*
Diameter 1–4cm, height 1–2cm

SYNONYM Bachelor Buttons.
DESCRIPTION Globular when young, soon
expanding into a shallow bowl or hemisphere.
The upper surface of the fungus is black and
shiny. When mature, it emits clouds of black
spores if disturbed; these are so dense that the
fungus is soon surrounded by a sooty deposit.
The exterior surface is brown and covered in
small warts. The flesh is firm and brown, leathery
in dry weather and gelatinous in wet weather.
HABITAT Grows in large clusters on the fallen
branches of oaks, Beech *Fagus sylvatica* and
Horse-chestnut *Aesculus hippocastanum*, inserting
its mycelium into cracks in the bark and causing
the wood to rot. Autumn and winter.
EDIBILITY Not edible.

Beech Jellydisc
▪ *Neobulgaria pura*
Diameter 0.5–2cm

DESCRIPTION This small,
lobed jelly fungus ranges in
colour from violet or purple to
grey or beige. Occasionally, pure
white specimens are found. The
cup- or vase-shaped fungus is
slightly bulbous at first, with an
inrolled margin displaying the
smooth exterior. As it matures,
it becomes flattened or concave
on top. The white flesh is fibrous
and pliable in dry weather, and
gelatinous in wet weather. The
stem, if it exists, is lateral.
HABITAT As its common name
implies, the Beech Jellydisc
grows mainly on the logs and fallen branches of Beech *Fagus sylvatica*. Jul–Oct.
POSSIBLE CONFUSION Can be mistaken for colourless versions of the Yellow Brain
(p. 138), but that species is more convoluted.
EDIBILITY Not edible.

Green Wood-cup

▪ *Chlorociboria aeruginascens*
Diameter <0.5cm

SYNONYMS Verdigris Elfcup, *Chlorosplenium aeruginascens*.
DESCRIPTION This beautiful elfcup is a distinctive, brilliant blue-geen. The little fruiting body is cup-shaped at first, becoming flattened or disc-shaped and very irregular. The surface is smooth or slightly wrinkled. The flesh is blue-green. The short stem is central or eccentric, and may be smooth or slightly curving.

HABITAT In small groups on heavily decayed broadleaf trees. Summer and autumn.
POSSIBLE CONFUSION The closely related *C. aeruginosa* is virtually indistinguishable, except that the flesh is orange or yellowish; some experts consider it to be merely a variety of Green Wood-cup.
EDIBILITY Not edible. Wood infected with the mycelium turns blue-green and was a feature incorporated into the decorative wooden boxes known as Tunbridge ware that were popular in the 18th and 19th centuries.

White Saddle ▪ *Helvella crispa*

Diameter 4–6cm, height 4–12cm

SYNONYM Common Brain Fungus.
DESCRIPTION Has a curved, convoluted, lobed, pale beige cap, exposing the wrinkled inner surface. The spore-bearing hymenium is on the outer surface and looks a little like folded chamois leather. The flesh of the cap is ochraceous and thin. The tall, sturdy stem is white at first, darkening to yellow in old specimens, and is deeply furrowed.
HABITAT In broadleaf forests, often on leaf litter. Late autumn.
POSSIBLE CONFUSION Elastic Saddle *H. elastica* is similar but smaller, and has no convolutions in the saddle-shaped cap. It is not edible.
EDIBILITY Edible, but use caution. In their raw state, all members of the genus *Helvella* contain haemolysins, substances that destroy the red blood cells, so must be thoroughly cooked before eating.

Elfin Saddle ■ *Helvella lacunosa*
Diameter 2–5cm, height 5–10cm

SYNONYM Black Helvella.
DESCRIPTION Species of the genus
Helvella are ascomycetes (fungi that bear
their spores in small sacs called asci),
even though they have a superficial
resemblance to the basidiomycetes, the
group containing most of the larger fungi.
The Elfin Saddle is similar in shape to
the White Saddle (p. 148), but the whole
fungus is much smaller, and the cap is
greyish or black, is not as wrinkled and
has more of a saddle shape. The tall stem
is furrowed and hollow, as in the White
Saddle. The spores are white.
HABITAT Under deciduous or coniferous
trees. Late autumn and sometimes into
winter.
EDIBILITY Edible only if thoroughly
cooked; blanching is recommended.

False Morel ■ *Gyromitra esculenta*
Diameter 10–15cm, height 4–6cm

DESCRIPTION This is another relative
of the morels and brain fungi. The cap is
very large and wide, irregular and swollen
in relation to the stem, with many brain-
like folds. It is dark reddish brown or
sepia, with an inner surface that is white
like the stem. The stem is thick, folded
and furrowed.
HABITAT In small groups on acid soil
among dead branches on the ground
under conifers, often at high altitude.
Spring.
POSSIBLE CONFUSION Round Morel
Morchella rotunda is also found in spring;
its cap is similar in shape but, like those of
all true morels, is pitted as well as folded.
EDIBILITY **Poisonous** despite its name,
especially if eaten raw or undercooked.

Orange Peel Fungus

■ *Aleuria aurantia* Diameter 6–10cm

DESCRIPTION This handsome elfcup could indeed be mistaken for a piece of discarded orange peel. The shallow cups are lobed and irregularly shaped. The spore-bearing hymenium inside the cup is bright orange in wet weather but pales to pink, or even white, in dry weather. The flesh is pinkish and fragile, but rubbery in wet weather. The stem is very short or absent. The white spores disperse in a cloud when the fungus is disturbed. Occasionally, a variety is encountered that has a golden-yellow hymenium and a white exterior.

HABITAT Often grows in large numbers on bare earth, especially on clay soil. Summer and autumn.

EDIBILITY Edible even when raw.

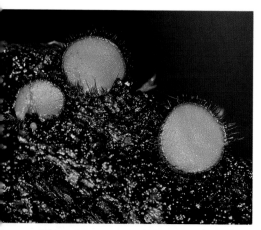

Common Eyelash

■ *Scutellinia scutellata*
Diameter 0.3–1cm, height 1–2cm

DESCRIPTION This tiny, disc-shaped red or orange fungus is easily overlooked. It is so called because it is edged with short blackish-brown hairs that look like eyelashes, although you will need a hand lens to see them clearly. The spore-bearing hymenium is on the saucer-shaped or concave area in the centre. The underside is darker. The spores are white.

HABITAT On buried rotten wood, in very damp soil such as in ditches and forests. Spring to autumn.

POSSIBLE CONFUSION There are actually several closely related species of *Scutellinia*, of which the Common Eyelash is probably the largest, but the only way to distinguish them is under the microscope.

EDIBILITY Not edible.

Coral Spot ■ *Nectria cinnabarina*
Diameter 2–4mm

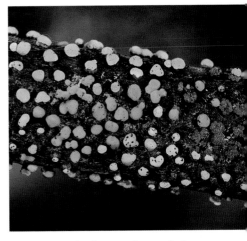

DESCRIPTION The conidial (asexual spore) stage of the species has a separate scientific name, *Tubercularia vulgaris*, and takes the form of tiny vesicles that cover tree branches in vast numbers; they are coral-red when young, darkening almost to the colour of their woody host. The vesicles are succeeded by orange-red sexual fruiting bodies known as perithecia, which form in groups around the conidial stage. The perithecia are globose, approximately 0.4mm in diameter, with a rough outer wall and a small pore at the tip.
HABITAT Coral Spot is a plant pathogen on broadleaf trees. Asexual spores appear in the spring, but the fungus grows year-round in huge numbers on the host.
EDIBILITY Not edible.

Morel ■ *Morchella esculenta*
Cap 3–7cm, Height 5–15cm

SYNONYM M. *vulgaris*.
DESCRIPTION The morels are ascomycetes, meaning that the spores are held inside small sacs (asci), so even though they superficially resemble a classic mushroom, they are not from the same family. The common or true Morel has a large round or oval grey to brownish cap that is covered in deep pits all over its surface. These pits, which may be edged with red, contain the asci. The white stem is also irregular and pitted.
HABITAT In damp woods, parks and gardens on sandy soil and burnt places. Spring.
EDIBILITY Edible and delicious but must be cooked. The Morel is as highly prized as truffles, and is sold fresh and dried in markets and groceries.

Semifree Morel

■ *Mitrophora semilibera*
Cap 3–4cm, height 10–15cm

SYNONYM M. *hybrida*.
DESCRIPTION This morel is very
distinctive in appearance, with a small
brown or olive pyramid-shaped cap. The
margin is clearly free of the stem. The cap
is covered in pitted folds (as in all morels),
which have a clearly defined darker edge.
The folds start at the top of the cap and
descend to the margin. The thick white
stem is furrowed at the top and has several
irregular folds. It is also granulose and
hollow, penetrating right inside the cap.
HABITAT In cool places, mainly under
poplars, but also found under elms and
Ash *Fraxinus excelsior*. Spring and summer.
EDIBILITY Edible only when cooked, but
decays quickly so must be eaten soon after
picking.

Blistered Cup ■ *Peziza vesiculosa*
Diameter 2–5cm, height 3–10cm

SYNONYM *Aleuria vesicularia*.
DESCRIPTION One of the largest elfcups,
with a receptacle that has a very incurving
rim, even at maturity. The interior spore-
bearing surface, or hymenium, is wrinkled
and is a pale ochraceous yellow, whereas
the exterior is pale brown and covered in
blisters. Sometimes the cup folds in on
itself and becomes the shape of an animal's
ear. There is a short stem, which is the
same colour as the exterior. The spores
are white.
HABITAT In large clusters that are
sometimes packed together on horse
manure and other dung, as well as on
well-manured soil, compost heaps and in
gardens. Spring to summer.
EDIBILITY Edible but not of interest.

Hare's Ear ■ *Otidea onotica*
Diameter 2–5cm, height 3–10cm

SYNONYM Ear-jack Fungus.
DESCRIPTION The ear shape of this
fungus is the reason for its common
name. The colour varies from yellow-
orange to ochre, or even fawn on the
outside. The outer surface is downy at
first, becoming smooth when mature.
The interior, covered with the spore-
bearing hymenium, is pinkish or orange.
The thin flesh is fawn-coloured, and
brittle yet elastic. There is often a short
stem, though this is occasionally absent.
If the stem is present, it is covered in a

thick, downy coating. The mycelial cords may be seen at the base.
HABITAT Usually under broadleaf trees, especially oaks. Less common under conifers.
Summer and autumn.
EDIBILITY Edible but of no culinary value.

Scarlet Elfcup
■ *Sarcoscypha austriaca*
Diameter 2–5cm, height 1–3cm

DESCRIPTION These elfcups are shaped
more or less regularly, like the cup of an
acorn, bearing the spores on the inner
layer. The spore-bearing hymenium is a
brilliant, shiny red that looks as if it had
been painted. The outer surface is paler,
reddish at first, then fading to pink and
even off-white. The flesh is thin, pinkish
and leathery, and relatively insipid. The
red stem is very short to absent.
HABITAT Grows in small groups on
dead branches, especially of Hazel
Corylus avellana, on the ground, in
damp, shady places, buried under
moss or humus, and in hedgerows,
copses and damp undergrowth.
Late winter to spring.
EDIBILITY Not edible.

Candlesnuff Fungus

■ *Xylaria hypoxylon*
Diameter 2–5mm, height 3–8cm

DESCRIPTION This tiny fungus indeed resembles the wick of a candle someone has snuffed out, being black at the base and greyish white at the tip. The small, erect branches are cylindrical at first, later branching like the antlers of a Common Elk *Alces alces*. At the same time, they flatten, whitening at the tip as they become covered in mature spores. The base remains black and downy. When the fungus is fully grown, it loses its 'antlers' and becomes thread-like and completely black with a swollen upper part, like a burned-out match.

HABITAT Colonises in large numbers the cut side of logs of deciduous trees, especially Beech *Fagus sylvatica*. Year-round.

EDIBILITY Not edible.

Dead Man's Fingers

■ *Xylaria polymorpha*
Diameter 1–3cm, height 3–10cm

DESCRIPTION This small club fungus is irregularly shaped into twisted, erect branches that expand into swollen, club-like or lobed shapes at the tip, very much as the sinister common name describes. The texture of the spore-bearing layer, the grey or black hymenium, is felty or granulose, while the corky flesh underneath this layer is white. The spores are black.

HABITAT Grows in twisted clumps at the base of broadleaf trees, mainly Beech *Fagus sylvatica*. Year-round.

POSSIBLE CONFUSION There are 2 similar, closely related species, Dead Moll's Fingers *X. longipes*, which has more elongated 'fingers' with a rounded tip, and *X. digitata*, in which the 'fingers' are elongated and welded together.

EDIBILITY Not edible.

Cramp Balls
■ *Daldinia concentrica*
Diameter 5–7cm

SYNONYM King Alfred's Cakes.
DESCRIPTION These dark brown to blackish fungi, initially globose and later hemispherical, might be mistaken for the cakes King Alfred allegedly was supposed to watch but allowed to burn – hence their alternative common name. Their colour can vary from chocolate-brown to violet and shiny black. They are dense at first and covered in small pores known as ostioles. There is no stem. The spore-bearing surface is on the outside of the fruiting body and the black spores stain the surrounding wood as they mature. When the fungus is cut open, the flesh is seen to consist of soft, concentric silvery rings, interspersed with hard, dark rings.
HABITAT On rotten wood, especially Ash *Fraxinus excelsior*. Year-round.
EDIBILITY Not edible.

Wolf's Milk ■ *Lycogala terrestre*
Diameter 1.5cm

SYNONYM Toothpaste Slime.
DESCRIPTION This is a slime mould, or myxomycete, which some experts now claim are not true fungi. In the single-cell, plasmodial stage, it is able to move about and congregates with others by means of chemical signalling. It then forms clusters known as peridia or aethalia, cushion-like pink globes that are slimy when young and contain a pink paste if broken open before maturity. They darken when mature, as they are covered with a purplish-brown to ochre spore mass.
HABITAT In large groups on rotten wood. Jun–Nov.
POSSIBLE CONFUSION Wolf's Milk Slime *L. epidendrum* is similar but has a grey spore mass and peridia. It is often found growing with Wolf's Milk.
EDIBILITY Not edible.

REFERENCES AND FURTHER READING

Breitenbach, J. and Kraenzlin, F. (eds) (1984–2005). *Fungi of Switzerland*. Vols 1–6. English edn. Edition Mycologia.

Buczacki, S. (1992). *Mushrooms and Toadstools of Britain and Europe*. HarperCollins.

Gminder, A. and Bohning, T. (2008). *Mushrooms and Toadstools of Britain and Europe*. A&C Black.

Harding, P. (2006) *Mushroom Hunting*. Need to Know series. HarperCollins.

Harding, P. (2008). *Collins Mushroom Miscellany*. HarperCollins.

Harding, P., Lyon, T. and Tomblin, G. (2007). *How to Identify Edible Mushrooms*. HarperCollins.

Kavalier, L. (1965). *Mushrooms, Molds, and Miracles*. The John Day, Company; reprinted 2007, Lincoln, NE, in an Authorsguild Backprint edition, iUniverse, Inc.

Large, E.C. (1946). *The Advance of the Fungi*. Jonathan Cape.

Sterry, P. and Hughes, B. (2009). *Collins Complete Guide to British Mushrooms and Toadstools*. HarperCollins.

USEFUL ADDRESSES AND CONTACTS

British Mycological Society (BMS)
The Wolfson Wing
Jodrell Laboratory
Royal Botanic Gardens, Kew
Richmond
Surrey
TW9 3AB
www.britmycolsoc.org.uk
The BMS was founded in 1896 and now has some 1,400 members from many countries around the world. Its sole objective is to promote all aspects of mycology, the study of fungi. Anyone with an interest in mycology can join, making them eligible to attend meetings and forays.

International Mycological Association (IMA)
www.ima-mycology.org
Founded in 1971, the IMA has 30,000 members. Membership is open to societies and individuals. The association holds meetings all over the world, though mainly in the USA.

The Mycologue
40 Swains Lane
London
N6 6QR
www.mycologue.co.uk
Sells all types of mushrooming equipment, including field guides.

Royal Botanic Gardens, Kew
Richmond
Surrey
TW9 3AB
www.rbgkew.org.uk
One of the aims of the Royal Botanic Gardens is to expand knowledge of plants and fungi, including taxonomy, through science and research. Its website includes valuable resources, useful to anyone interested in learning more about fungi.

▪ INDEX ▪